Library of
Davidson College

HUMAN VALUES IN A SECULAR WORLD

Edited by

ROBERT Z. APOSTOL
Creighton University

HUMANITIES PRESS
New York   1970

© *Copyright 1970 by*
Robert Z. Apostol

Library of Congress catalog card number, 76-135530
SBN number 391-00120-5

ACKNOWLEDGMENTS

The editor wishes to express his sincere appreciation for the cooperation of the contributors of the essays that appear in this volume. Words of thanks must also go to Dorothy J. Heise, Albert J. Kollasch, Sister M. Catherine Rupp and Reverend Joseph D. Scallon, S.J. for their procedural and style recommendations; to Judith Coughlon, Sister Stephanie Matcha and Barbara Pound for their assistance in reading galley and page proofs; to David J. Thompson for other technical assistance.

The editor is grateful to Edward G. Warin and the other students, colleagues, administrators and alumni of Creighton University, Omaha, Nebraska, for their interest in, and support of, this venture. Likewise, he is thankful to the members of the University's Philosophical Society, including those from all participating institutions: the interdisciplinary character of their orientations played a significant role in inspiring the idea of the Institute on Human Values.

Robert Z. Apostol

Creighton University
Omaha, Nebraska

FOREWORD

In a day when the values of the establishment are being challenged by youth, those of religion by a secular world, those of capitalism by communism, and those of rationalism by empiricism, it is important that we reflect seriously about values—not just values that are workable for a single social group but those which need to be universally accepted. Professor Apostol, in arranging this series of lectures, has performed a significant service for Creighton University and the Omaha community, and now by having the lectures published he is making available to the general public material which can stimulate our society to recognize both the importance of a consideration of human values and the tensions which occur between competing value systems.

As I am travelling in Europe I am made acutely aware of differing customs and value standards. Many of these differences add richness to the human scene, and they need to be preserved. On the other hand, there are also some overarching values which need to be recognized by all mankind if man is going to survive. More specifically, certain values need to be generally accepted if man is to avoid annihilation by war or environmental pollution. Furthermore, in view of automation it seems evident that some values need to be affirmed if man is going to avoid dehumanization.

The lectures in this series point to the need of acceptance of these universal values. They also bring to mind questions man is asking as to whether these universal values can be supported by reason, by reference to a divine or transcendent order, by situational awareness, or merely by man's practical concern for survival. In times of uncertainty these questions should be considered soberly and rationally. It is not time for dogmatism or violence. I trust that the publication of these lectures will stimulate such sober rational reflection.

Clifford T. Hanson
Professor of Philosophy
Dana College
Blair, Nebraska

CONTENTS

1. *Introduction*   1
   ROBERT Z. APOSTOL

2. *Religion in a Secular World*   11
   LOUIS DUPRÉ

3. *Value Scales and Today's Morality*   21
   VERNON J. BOURKE

4. *Existentialism and the Vision of Man as Person*   39
   GERALD F. KREYCHE

5. *The New Marxism and Human Values*   57
   RICHARD T. DE GEORGE

6. *The Time of Our Lives*   81
   MORTIMER J. ADLER

7. *The Future of the Moral Order*   111
   PAUL G. KUNTZ

INTRODUCTION

"Anxiety for the future time disposeth men to inquire into the causes of things: because the knowledge of them maketh men the better able to order the present to their best advantage."[1] Thus Thomas Hobbes, in the middle of seventeenth century, described human anxiety. While his description does not by any means bring out anything exclusively characteristic of our age, the habit of mind he analyzes appears to be responsible for the different brands of humanism that have gradually made their impact on our world today.

In our dealings with young men and women during the past decade, many of us have observed in them a genuine desire to reach out for values and an effort to grasp the human situation in this fast-paced, pressure-filled, though otherwise meaningless, race euphemistically called *human* existence. A temporary philosopher, J. Glenn Gray, once made an astute observation which I think characterizes the mood we now witness. "Lacking an embracing cause and a fervent ideology," he writes, "the student's search for a durable purpose is likely to become aggressive, extremist, at times despairing."[2] This mood makes sense because it seems to stem from that feeling of emptiness which results when a human person has nothing to live for but a vaguely understood self. I strongly suspect that the conflict we detect in our period of history is rooted in men's attempt to break the impasse between the problems of one's self and those of others.

Our present human condition has taught us a lesson which may well have given a new direction to our search for knowledge and even truth. People—in and out of academic communities—recognize that knowledge can become intelligible only if related to the concrete realities and human imperatives of our times. That is why men continue the search for human values in spite of the confusion arising from the current uncertainties. The sensitivity reflected by young people to the problems of contemporary society seems to indicate a conscious, intimate involvement with men's search for truth and the values they profess to discover.

It is not unlikely that the very uncertainty of the existing values in our society has generated a kind of secular idealism which seeks to respond to the unresolved problems of our times. The apparent apathy toward meaningful religious expressions, the double standards employed in various orders of social life, the realization of selfish aims at the expense of the underprivileged strata of society, the conflict of values determined by major powers, the inability of alienated segments of society to exercise and develop human freedom, and the place, if any, of the moral order in this constantly changing modern existence—these and other factors have actually made our confused age even more sensitive to human values. Defying the perennial distinction between intrinsic and instrumental values which scholars have sought to maintain, the modern mind appears to recognize a human value as one related with a problem that men must solve to better the human condition.

At a period of history such as ours, professional philosophy must recall the classic admonition recorded by Plato in Socrates' *Defense*, that "the unexamined life is not worth living." Philosophy must accept this dictum as a self-evident premise if it hopes to exert any meaningful influence on the solutions of today's gradually shrinking world. That life without some sort of examination is not worth living is perhaps more true today than in the time of the Greek thinkers, and there is less reason for Socrates to apologize that "it is not easy to convince you of it."[3] The present condition puts our mode of thought to a test to see that our ideas reflect the philosophical concerns of an age marked as much by unrest as it is by scientific discovery.

An eminent American philosopher recently made an observation which suggests that he, for one, is thoroughly convinced of the need of this sort of examination on the part of professional philosophers if they are to fulfill their avowed purpose of communicating thought to the society of which they are a part. Robert J. Kreyche attempts to give a characterization of the brand of "timidity" which the thinkers of present day America appear to manifest:

> Most of the philosophers in the United States today, in their desperate attempt to establish a scientific method for their studies, have reduced philosophy to a concern for logic and language. They have failed to respond to the modern world, and they have failed to provide a practical philosophy for it—practical in the sense of addressing itself to the problems of war, poverty, violence, and crime, or practical in the deeper spiritual values that lie at the base of American culture and life.[4]

This comment by a contemporary thinker, is not merely a perceptive and accurate description of the state of philosophy; it also appears to call in question William James' mild slur on Pierce's "Principle of Pragmatism" as being of merely topical value. "By that date (1898)," he said, "the times seemed ripe for its reception."[5] The term "pragmatic" was widely talked about. Perhaps the needs of our times will make our decade—and the next—better prepared for the pragmatic method, which has been defined by James himself as "the attitude of looking away from first things, principles, 'categories', supposed necessities; and of looking towards last things, fruits, consequences, facts."[6] In spite of the so-called "pragmatism" of William James and John Dewey, Robert Kreyche's statement seems to question the truly pragmatic character which has been attributed to American philosophy and is said to be "peculiar to American civilization."[7]

The era in which we exist has created the climate along with the imperatives that not merely put our ideas to a test but also force us to speak of human values in a realistic, workable way. For this reason, when I conceived the idea of setting up the Institute on Human Values in the fall of 1968 at Creighton University, I thought of inviting some of our scholarly thinkers to address themselves to important moral issues of contemporary society with an eye to highlighting those values that are at the base of human life today. In spite of the plurality of their approaches, I am fully convinced that the thinkers represented in this present volume have done more than establish the existence of universal human values. They have demonstrated the relevance of these values by showing how they operate in people's lives in our times.

Louis Dupré of Georgetown University is concerned with the issue of making religion intelligible in a secular world, i.e., a world in which there appears to be no room for the sacred. He suggests that the "emancipation of human values from their religious basis is the essence of secularization." Yet, in the process of becoming aware of his freedom, his control over his environment, his creative influence even on what is banal in life, man is similarly confronted with his own contingency. And by a strange paradox of today's human condition, man is compelled to recognize the sacred in the very experience through which he seeks to liberate himself. The anguish which accompanies man's realization of his lack of existence forces him to search for what comprehends his very being. Dupré feels that the anxiety that man experiences today plays a positive role in realizing the religious in him. This awakens in us important questions we ask ourselves. Could the conflicting problems brought about by secularism generate a stronger and more meaningful faith in the people of our times? Does man, in fact, continue to reach out for the sacred in and through the profane?

Vernon J. Bourke of St. Louis University surveys various alternative approaches for the construction of a scale of values in which the justification of man's moral decisions must be rooted. He makes a very good case for the need of a better understanding of man's abilities and his relationships to other parts of his real environment, if it is indeed imperative for man "to set up and defend a table of standards" through which he can recognize the hierarchy of values involved in all moral judgments. He points out failures in modern social sciences to provide such needed knowledge of man and demonstrates the present inability of contemporary philosophy to justify any scale of values. He rightly observes, however, that it is expedient for contemporary man to go by his present knowledge of man while he strives to construct value scales that will be both significant and workable.

Gerald F. Kreyche of De Paul University offers a defense of existentialism, which admittedly needs one, for it is not unncommon to hear confused people ask, "Must I lead a bad life to be an existentialist?" G. Kreyche attempts to vindicate the unsystematic philosophical approach by suggesting that "it is not mere existence which is the interest of existentialism; it is *human* existence." Stressing that it is against abstractionism in philosophy that the movement protests, he surveys the panorama of existentialist philosophy to bring to light its contribution to our modern understanding of man as a person who must be accepted as one revealing himself within constantly expanding horizons, because "to be a person is to be authentic." Such an approach enables us to understand such human experiences as faith and love, not to mention the values they assist us to recognize.

Richard T. De George of the University of Kansas ably

makes use of the Soviet invasion of Czechoslovakia as a take-off for a discussion of a possibility of a universal human morality in spite of "official morality," Marxist or otherwise. He develops the proper relationship among the three types of morality in a society, i.e., official morality, conformity morality and autonomous morality. The realization of a universal human morality on any of these three levels seems impossible and undesirable, because of the variety of ends people set for themselves and because "those who believe they have found the true human morality or the truly universal human values, have no right to impose their views upon any other individual or group." Fully realizing the difficulties of finding a way of determining the best morality, De George indicates that "the way of prudence lies in accepting the moral least common denominator which will render communal life on a global scale tolerable."

Mortimer J. Adler, director of the Institute for Philosophical Research, deals with what he regards to be the basic moral choice of man: "the choice between having a good time and leading a good life." After describing what he means by "a good life," he attempts to show that "this is the best century to be alive in." It would be difficult to find many who can say with Adler's conviction that Aristotle's *Ethics*, upon which his development is completely based, "is the only sound, practical solution to the problem" of leading a good life as a moral imperative. After posing the question of what is required to make the moral choices we ought to make, Adler proposes "moral virtue," which he explains to mean, "a habitual disposition to prefer a good life to a good time." Having established this premise for moral values, he proceeds to suggest that the ideal society is one which actively provides its members with the external conditions they need and encourages them in their effort to pursue a good life. After describing the advances some 20th century nations have realized, which have made them vastly superior to any previous societies, he offers certain observations about how a value system can undermine the pursuit of a good life even in a society such as that of the United States where the external conditions conducive to the "good life" appear to exist to a greater extent than at any other time or place.

Paul G. Kuntz of Emory University surveys the moral concerns of contemporary society. He tries to show that "we do not have any longer a single moral order," and he maintains the proposition that two opposing moralities seem to be developing. He contrasts the morality of the meritocracy, in which professionals become increasingly powerful and tend to dominate and control the future, to the moral attitudes of the rest of society. He further shows that the social structure is technocratic, concerned with the mastery of complex bodies of learning, while the culture appears to emphasize pleasure, permissiveness and distrust of authority and of the designs of a technological world. This polarization of the two moralities is distressing because society needs consensus about values if it is to endure and cultivate certain goals. Kuntz suggests that the two moralities can survive only "by making themselves intelligible to each other," and he feels that this end is attainable through agreement on four principles: 1) that it is good to satisfy needs, 2) that life is sacred, 3) that it is right to be honest, and 4) that violence should be avoided. It has been observed that the effort Kuntz makes to bridge the two moralities is admirable and very important, but that the adequacy of the four common principles he proposes is open to question.

These scholarly papers reflect the thoughts of a few distinguished thinkers in our contemporary society. They confirm what appears to be a truism: that in his constant quest for greater self-understanding, contemporary man realizes that he must be a questioner in the world, that he must make an effort to reconcile values, the timely with the timeless. In this on-going process of moral searching during a period characterized by anxiety, this institute has addressed itself to significant issues of the present day: religious, personal and ideological. These essays, too, definitely confirm Jacques Maritain's conviction that "human sciences . . . afford us with invaluable and ever-growing material dealing with the behavior of individual and collective man and with the basic components of human life and civilization," which thoughtful men today must certainly utilize as "an immense help in our effort to penetrate the world of man."[8]

I am proud to offer these reflective contributions to the public in this volume, for they manifest a quality which ought to characterize the philosopher of our times, the courage to develop and effectively communicate ideas that society needs. "Ideas," Robert Kreyche says, "are the result of persistent labor, effort, and creativity of the sort that demands an unusual courage to bring them to light."[9] The men whose papers appear on these pages have had not merely the courage to come up with needed ideas but the ability to make themselves intelligible to people of different interests in our pluralistic society.

If we are ever to achieve "an orderly world," we must somehow learn to appreciate the wisdom of the biblical assertion that "there is a time for every purpose under the heavens." (Eccles. iii: 2) Our period of history is undoubtedly a time for a reaffirmation of human values to guide our personal and social lives. As Lady Wooton succinctly put it in her *Testament for Social Science*, "The contrast between man's amazing ability to manipulate his material environment and his pitiful incompetence in managing his own affairs is now as commonplace as it is tragic."[10]

It is the rightful expectation of everyone in our times that we professional philosophers speak about human values not merely in a way that can be understood but, more significantly,

INTRODUCTION

in a manner that will contribute to the betterment of the human condition. It is in the confident hope that the essays which appear in his volume will fulfill this expectation that this collection is offered to the public.

ROBERT Z. APOSTOL

Footnotes

[1] Thomas Hobbes, *Leviathan.* ed. Michael Oakeshott. New York: Collier Books, 1962. p. 85.

[2] J. Glenn Gray, "Salvation on the Campus: Why Existentialism is Capturing the Students," *Harper's*, Vol. 230, No. 1380, May, 1965. p. 54.

[3] *The Collected Dialogues of Plato.* ed. Edith Hamilton and Huntington Cairns. Bollingen Series LXXI. New York: Pantheon Books, 1963. p. 23, 38, a.

[4] Robert J. Kreyche, "The Timidity of American Philosophy," *The Center*, Vol. II, No. 4, July, 1969. p. 29.

[5] William James, *Pragmatism*, New York: Meridian Books (World Publishing Co.), 1965. p. 43.

[6] Ibid., p. 47.

[7] Gail Kennedy, *Pragmatism and American Culture.* Boston: D. C. Heath and Company, 1950. p. vi.

[8] Jacques Maritain, *On the Use of Philosophy.* Princeton: Princeton University Press, 1961. p. 10.

[9] Robert J. Kreyche, p. 29.

[10] London, 1950, p. 1. Quoted by Kenneth R. Minogue, *The Liberal Mind.* New York: Vintage (Random), 1968. p. 153.

RELIGION IN A SECULAR WORLD

Louis Dupré

During the last five centuries Western man has brought ever more spheres of existence under his control. Simultaneously with this conquest he has come to consider himself as his own creator of values. His awareness of creative autonomy has extended from the artistic and the technological to the scientific and presently even the moral sphere. It is this unprecedented awareness more than any factual development which is causing today's religious crisis. In the past, religion was the integrating factor of human existence, relating all values to a transcendent principle. A general feeling of dependence in a universe which dominated man more than he dominated it, made such a reference indispensable. But once he discovered that all power to control the world is within himself, the need to relate each value to a transcendent principle ceased to exist. This emancipation of human values from their religious basis is the essence of secularization. Bonhoeffer summed it up in the statement that everything gets along without God just as before and what we call God is being edged out of life altogether.

Can religion survive in a cultural environment which no longer needs it as an integrating factor? Even if one disagrees, as I do, with those who answer this question negatively, one cannot deny that traditional religion because of its close connections with an out-dated worldview is bound to suffer. This conclusion is confirmed by the actual regression of religious beliefs and practices in a secularized society. A few years ago a Communist sociologist, Erika Kadlecova, published a survey of the religious situation (both private beliefs and Church affiliation) in Czechoslovakia and compared the figures with the last previous survey made in 1946 (before the Communist takeover). While fully allowing for pressure exercised by an atheistic totalitarian government upon its subjects, one can nevertheless hardly escape the impression that religion's worst enemy is not persecution but the totally secular character of public life. Miss Kadlecova concludes her survey with the following theory: "It seems to me that the collected material justifies the hypothesis that the present regression of religion is connected with the loss of its integrating function. Religion has ceased to be an ideology on which society is built: it has become removed to the private spheres of life." (Erika Kadlecova, "Kirche und Gesellschaft. Ergebnisse einer soziologischen Erhebung in der CSSR" in *Disputation zwischen Christen und Marxisten*, München, 1966, p. 252.) In its secularity, at least, the socialist society is an image of the society of the future.

The question, then, returns: Can religion survive in a secular world? Secularity is an undisputable fact. For most of our contemporaries, including most believers, no particular sphere of existence can still be called sacred. They no longer *directly* experience the holy either in the world or in the mind. The outer world has become totally humanized, while the inner mind knows no experiences which could be called unambiguously religious. These are facts and the reasonable thing to do is to accept them.

On the other hand, it would be far from correct to assume that modern man is no longer concerned about the transcendent. The more man becomes aware of his own creativity, the heavier the contingency of the human condition as a whole seems to weigh on him. The more he appropriates the world, the more he seems to become alienated from himself. Frustration seems to grow with efficiency. It is true enough that Western man has attained an unprecedented control over his environment and that this conquest was entirely in line with genuine human aspirations as well as with his religious tradition. But the onesidedness with which man has pursued this goal makes one wonder whether the achievement was worth its price. Western man's unconditional commitment to the technical and the pragmatic has banalized life for the sake of controlling it.[1] Apart from those who speculate about the purely secular, everyone else seems to feel frustrated by this diminished life. More than ever people are turning their backs on a society whose only goal and purpose seems to be the "appropriation" of the world, whether it is defined in terms of Western, pragmatic materialism or in terms of Eastern, dialectical materialism. Drug addicts, alcoholics and an unprecedented number of neurotics are the witnesses to the limitations of a worldview which has covered up all transcendent vistas of existence.

The judgment of philosophers and psychologists on our time is less dithyrambic than that of some radical theologians. Heidegger considers the forgetfulness of the sacred—which he determines as *Being (Sein)*—a flight from authentic existence. The *fallenness* of man consists precisely in that he, distracted by the *beings (Seiende)* around him, forgets the mystery of his own presence-to-*Being (Dasein)*. This loss of the ek-static openness to the sacred is to some extent inherent in the human condition itself. Yet our own generation is further removed from the sacred than any other by its blind fascination with science and technology, its devaluation of language in the mass media, and its unbridled desire to conquer and to dominate rather than to respect. In the final analysis, then, man is estranged from the sacred because he is *alienated* from his own ultimate reality. The concept of alienation is as essential for understanding the religious situation of modern man as is Bonhoeffer's often quoted word that man "has come of age." The notion, fashionable among secular theologians, that man's development toward cultural autonomy closes off a transcendent dimension of his existence which was open in a previous stage, is a strange piece of Comtean evolutionism.

Alienation is a word too complex to define. It broadly implies that man has become a stranger to himself. The term received a philosophical content from Hegel who in the *Phenomenology of Mind* applied it to the divided self, the unhappy consciousness. Marx connected alienation with the industrial production process. Yet he unduly narrowed its scope by forcing it upon the Procrustean bed of an economic theory of man. The roots of alienation reach far beyond the social-economic conditions of life, to creative freedom itself turned into a power of destruction. Nuclear energy is being used for producing atom bombs, industry pollutes the sources of life, progress in medicine results in unmanageable population increases, cultural and technical progress leads to cluttered roads, omnipresent noise, and an enormous output of non-sense. Modern forms of alienation can be understood only as inversions of man's creative freedom.[2]

In anguish man becomes acutely aware of the threat which freedom constitutes to its own existence. Psychologically anguish may be considered a state of consciousness which reveals a conflict between structural elements of the personality.[3] But ontologically anguish is man's existential awareness of the non-being inherent in his being, of finitude "experienced as his own finitude."[4] Kierkegaard's definition of anguish as the self's dizziness before the void of its own freedom, and Heidegger's subsequent development of the "nothingness" revealed in anguish, are generally known.[5] If these analyses are correct, anguish is inherent to freedom itself, but man will feel it more as he becomes more aware of his creative and destructive potential. In our age when man has tested his power to destroy life altogether, anguish brings out as much the nothingness which freedom can create as the nothingness out of which it creates. In revealing existence as surrounded by nothingness anguish questions the ground of existence and raises the problem of an ultimate reality. Many therefore feel that anguish incites man to adopt a religious attitude.[6] To what extent this view is justified will be considered immediately. But it is obvious enough that an experience which often results from the demise of a religious worldview can hardly be called religious itself. The loss of a religious communion with the cosmos is one of the main causes of anguish. In the past, religious participation in the founding rhythm of the cosmos provided man with "paradigmatic solutions"[7] for his existential crises. Urban industrial societies exclude such a communion: they have converted the world into a mere object of knowledge and conquest.

Anguish in its acute form is seldom experienced and soon forgotten. Yet it does not disappear without leaving a trace. The sediment of anguish after it has ceased to be active is a vague feeling of not being quite at home, called *uneasiness*. It implicitly questions what we normally take for granted. Gabriel Marcel rightly describes it as a principle of self-transcendence, allowing us "to detach ourselves from the vise in which everyday life squeezes us with its hundreds of cares which end up by masking the true realities."[8] Again, uneasiness is no more religious *per se* than is anguish. It often is the very reason why religious beliefs and practices cease to be meaningful. The same is even more true of *frustration*. Far from being intrinsically religious, frustration usually leads to escape and, if that is impossible, to an attempt to live on a more superficial level of existence where the frustrating situation may be forgotten. Alienation by itself merely opposes and stupefies, while religion reconciles and enlightens.

Nevertheless, it is in the various forms of alienation that modern man is most frequently confronted with religion. They urge him either to assert his contingency as an ultimate or to profess his faith in an absolute ground of his being. Religion itself cannot exist without the need to overcome one's present situation, which in turn requires an awareness that this situation is in some respect undesirable. Kierkegaard once wrote that most people are not ready for Christianity's cure because they do not feel sick enough.[9] The same holds true for any religion to the extent that an essential moment of the religious dialectic is the consciousness of being estranged from the ground of reality. The *consciousness* of alienation, then, is *potentially* religious. I say *potentially*, because man is more than ever inclined to escape from the ultimate questions of existence into the purely technical and the pragmatic.

Yet insofar as he can not much longer postpone facing these questions, man may be closer to the sacred than he suspects.[10] This seems paradoxical, for the more man's existence is inauthentic, the more it excludes the sacred. But the religious consciousness itself because of its dialectical nature requires in some form or other, the presence of its opposite. The sacred needs the profane. A strong awareness of God's presence usually alternates with an equally strong feeling of his absence. One of the most important religious events for the Jewish prophets is God's withdrawal because of Israel's sins. No one is further removed from God than the mystic in a state of desolation. The speculative form of today's a-theism does not make it less religious *as long as it experiences itself as negative,* that is, as in some way unsatisfactory. To look for God and not to find him is a religious act inspired by belief in some ultimate reality.[11]

Secular theologians claim that modern man must seek the sacred in and through the profane.[12] If this means that for our secularized contemporaries the road towards the sacred leads through the *awareness* of the secular as profane, the statement is undoubtedly true. But if it means that the secular itself has now become the sacred, it is false. For when the distinction between ordinary (profane) and ultimate (sacred) reality disappears, the dialectic of the sacred, and thereby religion itself, ceases to exist. It is therefore important to distinguish the secular in itself from the negative *awareness* of it as the profane. The second is religious, the first is not.

Religion has almost entirely lost its integrating hold over society as such. On the other hand, it has become a factor of social integration beyond and often against established society, by sacralizing an unprecedented feeling of brotherhood and social responsibility. The new generation seems to be religious through a communion with man rather than through a communion with nature. At the same time their religion has become less contemplative and more action-oriented. The civil rights movement and the Peace Corps, the joy of togetherness, even sexual promiscuity takes on a religious aspect for many young people that leaves their elders quite puzzled. Unpredictable and often totally undisciplined as these new expressions may be, they are authentic forms of religion and not moral substitutes to fill a religious vacuum. Yet again, the awareness of fellowship is no more religious in itself than the sense of mystery or the consciousness of alienation were. The brotherhood of revolutionary cells, resistance movements and oppressed groups may as often as not turn against religion, at least institutionalized religion. For some, however, the fellow-man becomes "sacred" as the manifestation of an ultimate reality.

In none of the preceding descriptions of religion does man experience the sacred directly. Instead he gives a religious interpretation to an experience which presents itself in a questioning rather than in an assertive way. To modern man the experience preceding the religious act is one that invites decision rather than passive submission. The appropriate name for the religious act which is not preceded by a direct experience of the sacred, is *faith*.

Footnotes

[1] Strangely enough, for some secular theologians terms like pragmatic and technical seem to connotate unequivocal progress rather than ambiguous attitudes which must be carefully scrutinized. Their descriptions of the present situation are amazingly uncritical of the prejudices of their age. I agree with Murchland's critique of *The Secular City:* "Cox conveniently ignores a powerful body of sociological criticism (since Marx), as well as a significant psychological critique that has been building since the time of Freud.... Just as Cox largely ignores the alienation in society, so too he fails to take sufficiently into account its theological cognate, which usually goes by the name of sin. Pragmatism has not yet proven itself capable of dealing with either form of negativity in any convincing way." *The Secular City Debate*, ed. by Daniel Callahan, Macmillan, 1966, pp. 18-19.

[2] An interesting description of alienation which has little in common with Marx's plight of the industrial proletariat may be found in the Czech Marxist Jiri Cerny, "Zum Begriff der Entfremdung" in *Disputation zwischen Christen und Marxisten*, Munchen, Kaiser, 1966, pp. 111-131.

[3] See Juliette Boutonier, *L'angoisse*, Presses Universitaires de France, 1949.

[4] Paul Tillich, *The Courage to Be*, Yale University Press, 1960, p. 35.

[5] Soren Kierkegaard, *Begrebet Angest, Samlede Vaerker*, ed. by A. B. Drachmann, J. L. Heiberg, H. O. Lange, Copenhagen, Gyldendal, 1920-36, pp. 345-48: *The Concept of Dread*, transl. by Walter Lowrie, Princeton University Press, 1944, pp. 37-40. For comments, see Louis Dupré, *Kierkegaard As Theologian*, Sheed and Ward, 1963, pp. 54-56. Martin Heidegger, *Was ist Metaphysik?*, 7th. ed., Frankfurt, Klostermann, 1955, pp. 33-34; transl. by R. F. C. Hull and Alan Crick, "What Is Metaphysics?" in *Existence and Being*, p. 336.

[6] In an Epilogue to *What Is Metaphysics?* written in 1943 Heidegger expressed the idea that Being, which at that time he had already started to describe in terms of the *holy*, can be rediscovered only in anguish. *Was ist Metaphysik?* pp. 46-47; "What Is Metaphysics?" in *Existence and Being*, p. 355.

[7] Eliade, *The Sacred and the Profane*, pp. 210, 166, 202.

[8] *Problematic Man*, transl. by Brian Thompson, Herder and Herder, 1967, p. 142.

[9] *Papirer*, ed. by P. A. Heiberg, V. Kuhr and E. Torsting, Copenhagen, 1909-1948, $X^3 A 184$.

[10] Paraphrasing Heidegger Thomas Langan writes about this age: "It is

closest because it is 'farthest away'; the perfectly inauthentic is always a total parody on the authentic; and the greatest absence of the sacred, of the mysterious, of authentic Being makes this very absence of the authentic most evident." *Recent Philosophy* by E. Gilson, T. Langan, A. Maurer, Random House, 1966, p. 148.

[11] The following statement about Simone Weil applies to many of our contemporaries: "He who, seeking God, does not find him in the world, he who suffers the utter silence and nothingness of God, still lives in a religious universe: a universe whose essential meaning is God, though that meaning be torn in contradiction and the most antagonizing paradoxes." Susan A. Taubes, "The Absent God" in *Towards a New Christianity*, ed. by Thomas J. J. Altizer, Harcourt Brace, 1967, p. 107.

[12] A Dutch theologian wrote recently: "There is a positive content in the expression 'God is dead'. It implies a justified rebellion against the so-called objectivization of God within the Church's Christianity. . . . God and faith belong together. God has been detached from faith, however, and subsequently objectified and hung somewhere 'up there'." Robert Adolfs in *The Meaning of the Death of God*, ed. by Bernard Murchland, Random House, 1967, p. 88.

VALUE SCALES AND TODAY'S MORALITY

Vernon J. Bourke

A favorite problem for existential philosophers is that of the person torn between two mutually exclusive decisions, each good enough, and consequently puzzled as to which to do. Suppose that a young man has to choose between staying at home to care for a widowed mother and going to Africa with the Peace Corps. How can he make the better choice?

Jean-Paul Sartre's solution tells the young person to go ahead and choose—either way. Say he decides to abandon his mother and go abroad. This decision, as Sartre sees it, is self-justifying. In the very act of electing to join the Peace Corps, this young man shows that this decision is right for him under these precise conditions. By the very fact of choosing, he endows his choice with self-created values.

To me, however, this so-called existential solution seems but an evasion of the issue. I think there should be some way of making such moral decisions in function of some criteria of judgment which can be publicly justified. After all, there is another existential solution to this problem: shoot mother and then join the Peace Corps. Apart from the incidental illegality of the shooting (which might be covered up by a really clever boy) this answer is neat and logically economical. Yet no recognized thinker would advocate such a shooting, even though there is nothing in existential ethics to condemn it. In fact, that is why existential ethics is an impossibility. Sartre has said this: "The ethical problem arises from the fact that Ethics is *for us* inevitable and at the same time impossible."[1]

In what follows, I shall argue that ethics is not impossible, unless we accept initial restrictions on the subject which predetermine it to failure.

Many moral problems involve not so much the simple doing of good and avoidance of evil as a judgment concerning which of two possibly good objects should be chosen. Let us take another example. After finishing secondary school a bright girl has been awarded a full-time scholarship at a university in her home town. Her mother thinks she should continue her education but her father advises her to work in the family store where no more education is required. This may not seem to be a *moral* problem: the girl may go either way and both choices may be good. Yet this sort of option may determine whether the girl is a success or failure in life. It could be a turning-point in the life of this human being. Suppose the girl decides to enter the family business: is she then making the best use of her talents? How could she be helped to answer such a question as well as possible?

This brings us to the concept of a scale of values. We are to examine whether it is possible to set up and defend a table of standards of moral judgment, in which the higher values take precedence over the lower. Take the following simplified table as a basis for our discussion:

VALUE A is Intellectual Satisfaction
VALUE B is Sensory Enjoyment
VALUE C is Biological Survival.

Value A is taken as the highest and C as the lowest.

The items in this table are not necessarily moral values but such items as biological survival and intellectual satisfaction may function as criteria for making moral decisions, provided it be established that they are ranked in this order of importance. For instance, the familiar problem of whether to rescue first the mature scientist or the young mother from a rapidly sinking ship might be resolved in terms of this table by arguing that the scientist would have more to contribute to our highest value. Our present aim is to examine the methods available for erecting and justifying such a scale of values.

Of course we should distinguish between the question: "how does anyone know that intellectual satisfaction is superior to sensory enjoyment?"—and our question which is: "how may an expert presume to justify such a table?" The first question is a moral one; it deals with the sort of knowledge that all humans need in order to make personal decisions in life. Such moral knowledge is very practical and greatly to be treasured but not to be confused with ethics. The latter is more theoretical; its answers would involve a type of knowledge not immediately applicable to personal decisions but rather for those who presume to teach or advise others as to how moral judgments may best be made. I hope that this distinction will help us to avoid an over-simplified view of our problem: personal morality is not ethics.

Another simplistic approach to the ranking of values used as criteria for moral judgment leads to the multiplication of scales. It is not a satisfactory answer to our problem to say that values A, B and C are so ranked, because they are equivalent to, or depend on, values P, Q and R. Unless scale P, Q, R can be justified in some more evident way than scale A, B, C, there is no ethical advantage in introducing the second scale.

Let us turn, instead, to the available ways of establishing a scale of values applicable to morality. Six such approaches are known: 1) subjective intuition or preference; 2) societal approbatism; 3) religious approbatism; 4) scientific axiology; 5) idealistic value theory; and 6) naturalistic value theory.[2] It will become obvious, I think, that I regard some of the last named positions as superior to the first ones, although there is something to be learned from most of these schools of axiology.

The subjective approach to moral values rests on the claim

that every mature person has some experience within his own consciousness of what is morally good or worth while. Subjective awareness of value may be cognitive or emotive. The subjectivist says, in effect, "I experience the primacy or intellectual goods over sensory goods or biological goods—and that is enough for me." If a pure subjectivist, he will not attempt to defend his ranking before other thinkers. He may urge others to follow his view of what is valuable but his subjective knowledge or feeling are essentially incommunicable. Some British writers on ethics have used the following bit of doggerel to illustrate the private character of subjective experience.

> I do not love thee, Doctor Fell.
> The reason why, I cannot tell;
> But this I know and know full well,
> I do not love thee, Doctor Fell.

This does not tell us much about Doctor Fell but it does convey, in no uncertain terms, the speaker's dislike for Doctor Fell. However, he cannot give an account to others to justify his feeling. Transferred to the problem of ranking values, this sort of subjectivism would reduce to private preference. John Stuart Mill reports that Jeremy Bentham once wrote: "quantity of pleasure being equal, push-pin is as good as poetry!"[3] To this assertion that a child's game is on the same qualitative value-level as poetry, one might reply, "That is what you think." The subjectivist has no way to offer public evidence for what he professes to see so clearly, because his experience is not open to participation. Actually, few subjectivists attempt to rank values and we need not delay further on this sort of approach.

Societal approbatism does have a good deal to say about value scales. It boils down to the notion that every culturally developed society embodies a certain code of approved conduct. Part of such a societal code is a scale of values. To make such a set of standards available for ethical discourse, one has only to examine the going views of his contemporary society. In this manner, social studies provide practical norms for ethical judgment.

We find a simplified version of this position on values in a recent article on the meaning of the "gross national product" of the United States.[4] A. A. Berle, an economist, asks whether a set of values can be discovered which express what Americans ought to be and ought to do. With some indebtedness to a book edited by Sidney Hook,[5] Berle presents a list of ten such standards:

1) People are better alive than dead.
2) People are better healthy than sick.
3) People are better off literate than illiterate.
4) People are better off adequately than inadequately housed.
5) People are better off in beautiful than in ugly cities and towns.
6) People are better off if they have opportunity for enjoyment—music, literature, drama, and the arts.
7) Education above the elementary level should be as nearly universal as possible through secondary schools, and higher education as widely diffused as practicable.
8) Development of science and the arts should continue or possibly be expanded.
9) Minimum resources for living should be available to all.
10) Leisure and access to green country should be a human experience available to everyone.

Although he does not list them in order of importance,

Berle considers these a minimum set of values to which most people in the United States would now agree. What is more, he insists that "no American value-system can be real except as it expresses a common divisor of the thinking of 200 million Americans."

This, then, is a neat illustration of the basing of a code of values on societal approbation. It is not absolute but it is offered as a set of norms showing what you would have to prize if you propose to live today as a good American. In some sense, such a scale of value is like the rules of baseball: they are man-made and open to change but *as long as they are accepted by the majority, or by a dominant set, of the persons involved*, they require a certain type of conduct.

British social utilitarianism is another version of this view. Good individual conduct is judged by its consequences to English society as a whole. The greatest good of the greatest number means in the concrete what is in accord with the prevailing ideals of the British gentleman. Utilitarian ethics never originates the standards, or provides the values, for good living —it distills these ideals from the conventions of decency in England. To the extent that it is limited to the moral values in one national culture, such a position cannot criticize the moral situation in another and different state. This is why British ethicians found Nazi Germany so frustrating, and it is why they are powerless to condemn racism in some former British colonies. Since an ethics is better if it can appeal to all men, societal approbatism is not the best approach to our subject, but in default of a well-grounded philosophical ethics, utilitarianism is better than nothing.

A good many writers on ethics, perhaps most, take a third way to the justification of moral values. They claim religious approval for their standards. Whether or not they initially use value language, it is clear that each of the great religions of the world teaches a system of moral values. One of the greatest living Catholic thinkers, Jacques Maritain, holds that the only complete ethics is one that borrows its starting-points from Christian revelation. His latest ethical work affirms "the absolute primacy accorded by Christianity to charity-love in the scale of values relating to human life and conduct;" and he adds, "Our good acts are definitely good by virtue of the charity which animates them."[6] This is a clear example of a Catholic form of religious approbatism in axiology.

Similar positions are taken by some Protestant writers. Paul Tillich, the two Niebuhrs, Dietrich Bonhoeffer, Paul Lehmann, Anglican Bishops John Robinson and R. C. Mortimer,—all would base moral values on Scripture or on their personal awareness of the promptings of God's will.[7] The same would be true of the value systems in Judaism, Buddhism, Islamism, and other religions. Of course this very plurality of religious approaches to ethical standards is an initial source of difficulty. Catholic morality, for instance, may have little relevance to the devotees of a different religion. Indeed, religious writers on ethics often display a bitter antipathy for all but their own value scales. Even within one institutional religion there is frequent disagreement as to the precise status of moral values in relation to the divinity. Joseph De Finance shows how Christian moral philosophers have taken four different positions on this key problem of God and value.[8] Some say with Immanuel Kant that autonomous practical reason needs no foundation in God. A second group (including Gabriel Vasquez, Christian Wolff and Cardinal Désiré Mercier) hold that, once God's existence is metaphysically established, the moral order of values can be worked out deductively, in terms of human nature and reason. A third school (comprising many Scholastic ethicians—and possibly De Finance) teaches that moral values can be established philosophically but imperfectly, in terms of an analysis of human nature—but this group holds that a complete knowledge of values requires explicit reference to God as supreme Value. In the fourth place, some Christian writers think that a prior and explicit knowledge of God is needed before any moral values can be known with certitude. We can gather from this account that, even within the confines of Christianity, the relation of a value scale to God is not a matter of uniform agreement.

Within the context of Roman Catholic thinking on this matter, we are living through a disturbed period of query and criticism. Some writers argue that a radically new moral philosophy (indeed, a new moral theology, also) is now required. Still others seem to say that no set of moral standards, no scale of ethical values, can have a permanent place in Catholic decision-making. These are, I think, extreme positions but they serve to remind us of the wide-spread doubt among present-day Catholics that the old explanations and justifications of moral guidelines are valid. Such an attitude is not peculiarly Catholic; there is a general tendency in contemporary ethics to question the validity of a theologically based ethics.[10]

If there are difficulties inherent in an exclusively religious attempt to justify moral values, there is even less agreement among those who try to ground standards of behavior on science. It is a commonplace to say that pure mathematics and the hard sciences (such as physics and chemistry) are morally neutral. Even many social scientists carefully avoid any advocacy of values or norms. Yet some attempts at a scientifically based axiology are being made. The British ethician, W. D. Lamont, has tried to develop a general theory of value from the study of economic valuation. He has suggested interesting parallels between the way that things are judged "good" in business and in morals.[11] Yet the results of such procedure are not impressive. Many efforts to deal scientifically with valuation lead to conclusions that are somewhat remote from ethics. One social psychologist placed his subjects in a dark room and asked them to report on the movements of an unmoving point of light. After the passage of some time, all subjects reported more or less movement. When the reports of others were heard, most subjects adjusted to a common range; those who had reported extensive motion cut down on their estimates, and those who described less motion than others increased their estimates. The conclusion was that people tend to conform to the appraisals of others and even to adopt whatever is the apparent common denominator of standards of judgment.[12] Whether one may extrapolate from this to value theory and ethics is debatable. Generally speaking, social scientists provide much useful material for ethical discussion and illustration but few profess to offer justification for any particular set of values. As Gordon Allport puts it: "I agree with Professor Maslow when he says that the validating capacity of social science is still somewhat feeble."[13]

One philosophical school with a highly developed theory of moral values is found in twentieth-century German thought. Max Scheler's phenomenology, for instance, offers a definite scale of values based on personal intuition, partly cognitive and partly affective.[14] In the moral order, Scheler ranks values by means of three characteristics. Values are higher because of length of endurance, independence form the organism of the moral agent, and a distinctive personal quality. On this basis, Max Scheler described four levels of material (i.e. not formal) values. At the bottom are the pleasant and unpleasant; next come life values; above these are mental values; and at the top are the absolute objects of religious experience, the holy and unholy. Morally speaking, an action or attitude is preferable to the extent that it shares in a higher rather than lower value.[15] Such a position requires acceptance of the validity of phenomenological method (which, for many of us, has a certain quality of vagueness); however, it must be admitted that Scheler's approach deserves serious study.

This way of getting at value is modified and further developed in the ethics of Nicolai Hartmann. It is not easy to determine whether this thinker is a realist or an idealist but he has a very impressive ontology. The second volume of Hartmann's major work is wholly devoted to value theory and morality. He utilizes several different value scales.[16] Starting with a lower value such as justice, Hartmann rises to brotherly love, then to love of the most remote, and finally to the highest level, personal love. Similarly, when he begins with self-control or temperance, he ascends to bravery, then trustworthiness, and at the top to radiant virtue and personality. As far as Hartmann's method is concerned, these gradations are to be recognized through a "sense of preference." What is more distinctive is Hartmann's claim that there is no identity between the superiority and the strength of moral values. The lower values on his scale are actually the strongest ones. Thus Hartmann argues: "To sin against a lower value is in general more grievous than to sin against a higher; but the fulfillment of a higher is morally more valuable than that of a lower."[17] For instance, he would say that to take a man's life is a very serious moral offense but one has a greater obligation to promote by positive action the development of the arts than the feeding of the poor!

Hartmann's ethics is based on a quasi-existent world of ideal or possible objects. Moral values are held to transcend the ordinary objects of sensory and intellectual experience. Such an ontology brings us back to something like the Ideal Forms of Plato. It has a good deal of appeal to people whose minds are capable of rising above the limitations of physical existence but this kind of axiology rests on private intuition and feeling. Oftentimes the content of these intuitions is but a restatement of the ideals of western culture.

In the past few years, I have become more and more convinced that a naturalistic approach to the standards of moral judgment is most promising. In the narrow sense, ethical naturalism reduces to scientific axiology, or to an attempt to ground judgments of what is good or right on verification in terms of empirical sense date.[18] This is too restricted a position, to my mind.

In a wider sense any ethics is naturalistic which endeavors to understand "good," or any other moral category, in terms of factual knowledge of the agent and the context in which he lives and acts. When G. E. Moore condemned the "naturalistic fallacy," he said that this mistake consists in explaining the moral predicate "good" in terms of something else, such as personal pleasure or social utility.[19] For Moore, most of his predecessors in ethics had committed this fallacy. Aristotle, Thomas Aquinas, even William Ockham, and all advocates of a theologically based ethics would thus be "naturalists" in Moore's sense. I should like to support a naturalistic method in ethics and value theory which would be broader than that of American scientific naturalism (or of European positivism) and yet narrower than the "naturalism" which Moore condemned.

It is my view that one cannot determine what is valuable or good for man without making a thorough study of the makeup and abilities of man and of the relations that he has to other parts of his real environment. As I see it, the values that are morally significant are those aspects and potentialities of the surrounding universe which provide man with the opportunity for personal development and for the optimum use of his powers.

What is first of all required in this program is a better understanding of the kind of being that man is. I really don't care whether this is called human nature or not. It need not imply an absolute or unchanging essence but, in point of fact, I see little difference between the characters in the Greek poems and plays of twenty-five hundred years ago and the men of today. What is different is the world in which we live.

We need to make a more careful study of the distinctive activities in which contemporary man engages: human biological functions, sensory activities including feelings, intellectual cognition and appetitive reactions. In other words, there is still a place for the philosophy of man (or an analytical type of individual anthropology) to be used as a basis for ethics and value theory.

I would be quite willing to admit that what used to be called rational psychology retained a good many outmoded notions from the psychology of Aristotle and his medieval commentators. Yet we cannot expect to substitute for this the psychology of today. Freud's id, ego and super-ego, for example are hardly superior to the *libido, spiritus* and *ratio* in Augustine's trinitarian psychology. Nor are experimental psychologists much interested in giving an account of the whole man who is the moral agent. The tendency is to offer very accurate descriptions of smaller and smaller parts of man's psychic life. Every school of psychological research uses its own special terminology and this makes it hard for the philosopher to use psychological materials to form a more adequate conception of the integral moral agent. Yet this is the sort of work that would have to be done, I think, before we could speak with confidence on the sort of values that would appeal to, satisfy, and complement men today.

In traditional Scholastic philosophy man's psychic functions were divided into the cognitive and the appetitive and then each of these areas was described on two levels, the sensory and the intellectual. Thus, man was pictured as knowing various aspects of individual physical reality through sense perception and as knowing the general meanings and interrelations of the objects of sense experience by means of intellectual understanding. The objects of sensation were individual; those of understanding were primarily universal in character. I think it is still important to retain such a two-level theory of cognition—at least until someone shows rather clearly that it is wrong. Similarly, in the area of appetition there is a vast difference between sensual desire or aversion for an individual object and intellectual willing of a universal object. It is one thing to be hungry for a good steak and quite another thing to love peace. Those who say today that love is the whole story in morality might let us know whether they are talking about *eros* or *agape*. My impression is that much confusion besets contemporary moral discussions, because of a lack of awareness of various levels and varieties of affective experience.

Still more complicated features of man's psychic functions also deserve re-study, with a view to the provision of a more workable moral psychology. The condition known as voluntariness in older philosophies needs further examination. When a person is morally responsible for his action (or omission) that action is said to be "within his power," or such that it can be done or not. This is not quite the same thing as saying that such actions are free: voluntariness implies a certain knowledge of the action, an adoption of the act as one's own, plus a certain spontaneity in the manner in which the action issues from the agent.[20] Still another feature of man's moral equipment is habituation. Much recent thinking on habit formation still follows the lines of William James' outmoded physiological treatment of habits as groovings in the channels of the nervous system. Far from being such static automatisms, psychic habits are perfectants of the higher capacities of the agent. There is a surprising degree of sophistication in the Thomistic account of moral habituation and it deserves to be better known.[21] Not enough attention is paid to moral habits in current ethical thinking. Finally, the whole problem of moral motivation requires reappraisal. Studies that are being done now lie too largely in the applied field of how people may be induced to buy a certain commercial product, or how they may be discouraged from drinking to excess, or something like that. Much more vital to ethical discourse would be basic studies on the fundamental psychological character of motivation. Forty or fifty years ago, in Germany, psychologists were working on this sort of things.[22] The topic is not sufficiently pursued today.

Man also finds himself the subject of a multitude of relations to things inanimate and animate in his environment. Many of these relations are quite real, that is to say, they are existing connections between a man and something else, and they are there whether the man recognizes them or not. Some such relations have a vector quality: they represent various needs, tendencies or exigencies associated with man. A child's early dependence on its parents, for instance, is a very real relationship with obvious moral implications, both on the side of the parents and of the child. Such relations are empirically discoverable and verifiable; they are facts quite as obvious as any collection of sense data. They do not have to be natural (i.e. from birth); a business partnership is an agreement which is a legal fact with moral responsibilities attached. David Hume, of course, denied the reality of such relations and then wondered how one could derive an "ought" from an "is"—or a value from a fact. But Hume was simply wrong. Neither man nor the universe is a collection of sense data. No scientist and no practical man could operate on the basis of Hume's philosophy. It is time that contemporary philosophers in the English tradition were awakened from their dogmatic slumbers induced by a dose of over-restricted empiricism. Man's environment is endowed with values precisely because man is really related to many parts of the universe and to many other men. He really needs to use some of these, to deal with others, and to avoid still others. Unless he reacts to such values, man cannot live and function as a human agent.[23]

Value is a two-ended affair. When I am thirsty there is a

factual condition in me, physiological and psychic, which entails a desire for a liquid, such as milk, capable of satisfying this inclination. Objectively, the qualities of milk are observably suited to the satisfaction of this need in man. This is a value that milk has and sulphuric acid, for instance, lacks it. Potability is not, as such, a moral value but it becomes moral whenever it enters in any way into the domain of man's deliberated activity. That is to say, as soon as a person is able to reason about the way that he lives his life, then he must be concerned about values like the potability of milk and the non-potability of sulphuric acid. It is not only physiologically wrong to drink such an acid; under most circumstances it is morally wrong to do so deliberately. This is because a reasonable man can understand the unsuitability to his whole being of such an action. By simple extrapolation, one can also see that it is immoral to induce another person to harm himself by drinking acid. The moral values, and the "oughts," implied in the discussion of the foregoing example are not fictions added to the factual state of affairs. While not entities in themselves, these values and imperatives are really present aspects of other beings in relation to the moral agent. If, in the case of a sick man, milk is found to be a harmful drink, then in this case there is a disvalue attached to milk and there would arise a moral obligation to avoid drinking milk.

At the start we used a three-level value scale as an illustration: biological values at the bottom, sensory enjoyment in the middle, and intellectual satisfaction at the top. This is too simple a table, of course; an ethically useful scale would require more categories of value. One would have to think of some higher value than the satisfaction of understanding. A social dimension involving relations to other persons would be necessary. Even biological value might have to be divided into those adjunct aspects of vitality (such as beauty of person and physical strength) and the probably higher value of persistence in life. In any case, these values would be determinable, I have suggested, after a very thorough philosophical study of the moral agent in relation to his surrounding universe. No attempt will be made to present a fuller table of values here. My argument has been that we now lack in contemporary philosophy the theoretical framework that would justify a valuable scale. In more traditional terms, we have more work to do in the philosophy of man, and in the broader area of metaphysics, before we can provide an anxiological base for ethics.

Footnotes

[1] J. P. Sartre, *Saint Genet*, London: Allen & Unwin, 1964, p. 186.
[2] For a different survey of the possibilities, see W. S. Sahakian, *Systems of Ethics and Value Theory*, Paterson, N.J.: Littlefield, Adams, 1964. The fourteenth chapter of my *History of Ethics*, Garden City, N.Y.: Doubleday, 1968, offers some backgrounds.
[3] See "Mill on Bentham," in J. S. Mill, *Utilitarianism*, edited by Mary Warnock, New York: Meridian Books, 1962, p. 123.
[4] "What G N P Doesn't Tell Us," *Saturday Review*, Aug. 31, 1968, pp. 10-12, 40.
[5] *Human Values and Economic Policy*, New York: New York University Press, 1967.
[6] *Moral Philosophy*, trans. by Marshall Suther et al., New York: Scribner's 1964, p. 83.
[7] See for example, Paul L. Lehmann, *Ethics in a Christian Context*, New York: Harper & Row, 1963; and many articles in the new *Dictionary of Christian Ethics*, edited by John Macquarrie, Philadelphia: Westminster Press, 1967.
[8] *Ethique Generale*, Rome: Presses de l'Universite Gregorienne, 1967, pp. 198-200.
[9] Supporters of this view, according to De Finance, are Card. Louis Billot, Victor Cathrein and Leonard Lehu.

10 See Richard B. Brandt, *Ethical Theory*, Englewood Cliffs, N.J.: Prentice-Hall, 1959, pp. 56-82, for such a criticism.

11 W. D. Lamont, *The Value Judgment*, New York: Philosophical Library, 1955; see his earlier work, *The Principles of Moral Judgment*, Oxford: Clarendon, 1946. For another type of theory, using mathematical analysis, see Robert S. Hartman, *The Structure of Value: Foundations of Scientific Axiology*, Carbondale, Ill: Southern Illinois Press, 1967.

12 M. Sherif, *The Psychology of Social Norms*, New York: Harper, 1936; with the discussion in Brandt, *op. cit.*, p. 126.

13 "Social Science and Norms," in Louis Z. Hammer, ed., *Value and Man*, New York: McGraw-Hill, 1966, p. 229. See also, W. F. Dukes, "Psychological Studies of Values," *Psychological Bulletin*, 52 (1955) 24-50.

14 For a brief English analysis of Scheler's *Der Formalismus in der Ethik und die materiale Wertethik*, (Halle, 1913-1916) see E. Gilson, T. Langan and A. Maurer, *Recent Philosophy*, New York: Random House, 1966, pp. 126-129.

15 For further exposition of Scheler's ethical theory, consult W. H. Werkmeister, *Theories of Ethics*, Lincoln, Nebraska: Johnsen, 1961, pp. 252-267; and Ernest W. Ranly, *Scheler's Phenomenology of Community*, The Hague: Nijhoff, 1966.

16 *Ethics*, trans. by S. Coit, New York: Macmillan, 1932, 3 vols.; vol. II: *Moral Values*, p. 387.

17 *Ibid.*, p. 53.

18 For such a narrow naturalism, see Carl Wellman, *The Language of Ethics*, Cambridge, Mass.: Harvard University Press, 1961, 20-37.

19 This is the argument of the first chapter of *Principia Ethica*, Cambridge, Eng.: The University Press, 1903.

20 For some British work in this area, see: G. E. M. Anscombe, *Intention*, Oxford: Blackwell, 1957; Stuart Hampshire, *Thought and Action*, London: Chatto & Windus, 1959; and the anthology edited by Alan R. White, *The Philosophy of Action*, London: Oxford University Press, 1968.

21 G. P. Klubertanz, *Habits and Virtues*, New York: Appleton-Century-Crofts, 1965, puts the medieval theory into contemporary language.

22 Cf. W. Haensel, *Beiträge zur Strukturanalyse des Wollens*, Leipzig: J. A. Barth, 1939, pp. 83-160 on motivation research.

23 See the excellent development of this view, by one of my former students: Sister Theresa Clare Morkovsky, "Morality and Real Relations," *The Thomist*, XXIX (1965) 396-419.

EXISTENTIALISM AND THE VISION OF MAN AS PERSON

Gerald F. Kreyche

Introduction

Amid all the chaos in the world today, there is one persistent cry which is voiced by young and old alike and which crosses all geographic borders and religious divisions. That plea is to be recognized as a person. More and more we stress the need for inter-personal relationships, for recognition of each other's identity as a human being. This need grows increasingly acute and in direct proportion to our being hemmed in by technology, machines and systems control. To a large extent, the rebellion in the world at large is a symbolic protest in the name of freedom and can be understood (if not excused) as an attempt to thrust aside the dehumanizing forces of our times. In times of such crisis the hidden resources of man either come to the fore or are stifled, to be silenced perhaps forever. As Nietzsche once remarked, "That which does not kill me will make me stronger!"

Although the notion of person has been studied for some time at the theoretical level, we are only beginning to recognize its meaning in the practical order. We are only beginning to appreciate the existential implications of man's dignity. This recognition has given rise in part to the movement of existentialism. Existentialism in turn has furthered this concrete vision of man as person, and it is this specific contribution I would like to elaborate in this paper. Let us briefly review the history of person in order to gain perspective for our theme.

Historical Development of the Person

As we know, in antiquity, person (*prosopon*) referred to the masks worn by actors in a play, signifying comedy or tragedy. Man was not the person, but the shadowy figure behind the mask or person. In Rome, person was identified with the free man. His chattel, the slave, was not free and therefore not a person. In western philosophy and in Christianity, lip service was paid to man the person, but it wasn't really *man*, as much as it was his *soul*, that received all the attention. It was man's soul that was regarded as the *real* person, the inner man. Even the liturgy of the Church today bears witness to this view when our prayers ask, not that *we* (our person) will be healed, but that our "souls" be healed, that our "souls" rest in peace, etc. The liturgy still suggest that our main concern is not the salvation of man, but the salvation of souls. When the body of man comes into consideration (if at all), it is treated only as an appendage.[1] All language about man bespoke a bifurcation, a dualism of mind and matter, of soul and body, of form and matter or of substance and accidents. Tribute was always paid to man's unity, but it was his soul which was of virtually exclusive concern.

Aquinas recognized the problem and refused to accord the status of person to the separated soul. For Aquinas, the soul of man was a substantial form and to prove that this *form* was immortal was not to prove threby that *man* was immortal. Strictly speaking, then, using the ideas and language of Aquinas, one does not pray for the poor persons in Purgatory, but for the poor substantial forms there! Immortality of the soul did not guarantee immortality of the person, but only of an element of the person. Hence to speak of personal immortality as proven in the philosophy of St. Thomas is to be ambiguous. Yet generations of "manual-fed" philosophers were nurtured on that ambiguity with the consequence that "like" continued to produce "like."

What also blocked out the view of man as person, was the institutionalism of previous ages. With this institutionalism was an overriding concern for the common good to the detriment of the good of persons. The legalisms dramatized in *Billy Budd, Les Miserables* and perhaps *The Deputy*, provide classic examples of conflict between the common good and the good of persons. It did not take long before the common good was identified with the good of the vested interest, with the good of the establishment.

Now, our age is an age which believes that the institutional good is best served through attention to the *bonum personae*, and it is on the person that we focus our attention today. This is witnessed in civil, religious and academic life. With this new emphasis, we see a priority of right over obligation, of persons over Institutions, of collegiality over a more efficient autocracy, and perhaps of freedom over certain forms of knowledge. But what role has existentialism had to play in all this? To answer, it would be helpful to "zero in" just a bit on what existentialism is, then to explore an existentialist view of man.

Existentialism: An Attempt at Clarification

Strictly speaking, existentialism cannot be defined, for it crosses several philosophical genera and species. But it can be described and its major features pointed out. Briefly, some of these are: its point of departure, and the pivot around which all its views center, is man—man as he exists in the world of history, where he dwells in his lived world of everydayness. Such a world is clearly juxtaposed to the many other worlds in which he momentarily resides, namely, the world of *techne*, the world of commerce, the world of politics, the world of the lecture hall—all the latter, being world where we each play our Wittgensteinian games. Consequently, it is not mere existence which is the interest of existentialism; it is *human* existence. Its methodology is phenomenology, the description and constitutive disclosing of that which appears. Its view of man is holistic, though no language can do full justice to this. Focusing its attention on those human aspects of man's birth, life and death, which help reveal man to himself, existentialism (sometimes against the will of the existentialists) is closer to biblical and semitic thinking than to traditionally accepted Greco-Roman modes of thought. It seeks to break out of restricted categorical thinking and away from the dichotomies on which such thinking feeds (and feuds).

Existentialism represents therefore a protest against the world of abstraction in philosophy and considers itself a humanism. To emphasize its concern for the concrete, it often stresses truth as value,[2] and the meaningfulness of love and action over speculative knowledge. Its vocabulary is that of literateurs. Such a vocabulary finds itself dealing with anxiety, despair, guilt, hope, love, mystery, crisis, etc. Yet existentialism is not interested in the words as such. Paraphrasing Plutarch, we can say, it is not by the knowledge of words that we come to the understanding of things, but by our experience of things that we are able to follow the meaning of words.

The experiences to which existentialism points are not the private domain of professional philosophers, but in the public domain of everyman. Perhaps we should not say more at this point, for beyond this, existentialists differ widely, even with respect to whether or not they are existentialists.

Setting an Existential Mood

The preliminaries out of the way, let us examine the vision of man offered through existentialist eyes. To do so, we must set for ourselves an existential mood, by reflecting on various aspects of human existence. This will prove more helpful than attempting a definition of man, for to define is to set limits and to restrict the openness we must have in order to see man as man. Further, this "existentialist vision" of man as person, reveals an indebtedness to many existentialists. Consequently, it belongs to none exclusively. Our efforts are not directed so much to an exposé of some particular philosopher's doctrine; rather we are attempting to "catch" an existentialist approach to a philosophy of man. Such an approach can only be sketched. Each of us must flesh it out, drawing from our own experiences. To create such a sketch, let us examine six existential experiences of man. These are 1) being born; 2) freedom; 3) *Angst;* 4) knowing; 5) friendship; and 6) death. A short consideration of these will help us point to man, letting him reveal himself to ourselves. Hopefully, it will provide us with the framework for an existential vision of man as person.

Being Born

If we reflect on the phenomenon of being born, we see that it is a traumatic and radical thrust into existence. It is a thrust into a world I did not choose and in which I experience a fundamental "thrownness' (*Geworfenheit*) and a sudden realization of my newly found being (*Befindlichkeit*). In this world, I first encounter myself as an object among other objects. I am not yet fully a person, I only have the potentiality for becoming one. That potentiality is a kind of nothingness at the heart of my being. It is this nothingness, this lack of complete determination that is one with my freedom and which I must choose and use to become more than a man. I must use it to become a subject, a person, to experience *human* existence rather than mere being. Nothing is characteristic of this human existence, only the inept language that futilely attempts to describe it.

At first I believed myself to live in the category of *das Man, der Mensch*, or in the realm of the editorial "we," of the "one" in the expression, "One never knows." But to understand myself in this category is to confuse myself with humanity at large, where while I become something infinitely great (quantitatively), I am at the same time (qualitatively) nothing at all.[3] However, I gradually begin to experience myself as the *moi*, the *Ich*, or as the child says, the me, myself and I. I see myself as I am, in my human existence as subject, rather than as others tend to see me as another being in the land of objects.

Cast into existence, I am told that I am free and therefore responsible. Here I first sense the irony of my facticity, for my freedom is everywhere given, except with respect to its foundation, for I had no choice in saying whether I wanted to be. The basis of my freedom lay entirely in some else's determination. Never consulted about whether I wanted to "carry the ball," I was only told, "You have it! Now you must run with it, or be tackled by the forces of opposition—the world of things." (This is what Sartre means when he says that existentialism is an activism. Whatever we do, we must act, we must choose!)

Our existence and our freedom strike us as absurd. Yet both are unquestionably facts. Both are strangely empirical, yet having no fabrication from the empirical world of objects. Let us take a hard look at this freedom which I rightly claim for my own.

Freedom

Freedom contains both negative and positive elements. To stress the negative, I might proclaim a kind of sin mysticism with Baudelaire and the school of "evil masters." This sin at least is mine—all mine! To stress only the positive aspects of freedom is to lose sight of the *Angst* accompanying every free act which must be marked by a note of uncertainty about itself.

Consider, for example, the way we view our freedom *before* we act, *while* we act, and *after* we have acted. This uncertainty, coupled with the necessity for decisions, resolutions and action, point unmistakably to man's finitude. This freedom wants to establish itself as its own ground, yet its finitude rules out this false triumphalism. Pride and despair, rationalism and nihilism, both find their origins in this fundamental experience. Sartre's discussion on man's "passion to be God," and Camus' pondering of suicide (for him, the only truly philosophical question), attest to this. Thus to be a person is to be authentic, and to be authentic, I must choose freedom. I lapse into "bad faith" (*mauvais foi*) if I allow myself to be free of this freedom, for in my human nature I am "condemned to be free."[4]

Herein lies both my glory and my shame. For through my freedom I create values. But to choose and create values is to be responsible and with responsibility comes *Angst*. Hence I now realized that existential man is *homo anxious*—the man of anxiety.

Angst

The existential anxiety at the heart of man can be seen in the difference between the philosophical and methodological doubt of Descartes versus the existential doubt that each of us harbors about ourselves. The first reveals a hidden confidence that betrays and renders impossible any real doubt in Descartes' philosophy. But the doubt we have about ourselves is existential and real precisely because it cannot stomach the dishonesty of such a false confidence. It is a doubt about the confidence and good faith themselves, about ourselves as human beings. Indeed, it is a reflective doubt about doubt itself.

This *Angst* and tension reveal man's uncertain nature, a nature that is always becoming and therefore never fully constituted. Kierkegaard understood this tension when speaking of faith. If we are sure we have faith, we can be sure we do not have faith. Whoever is certain that he is a Christian is certainly not a Christian.[5] Yet while none of us is a Christian, we can all be on the way to becoming Christians.

Angst (anxiety or dread) is fundamentally different from fear. Fear is always specific, having to do with this or that object, e.g., a fear of elevators, a fear of crowds, a fear of high places. *Angst*, however, is a condition that pervades man's entire being. It has no specific object, but is a reflection of the "nothingness" within man. It is the uneasiness characterized by the Viennese logotherapist, Viktor Frankl. It comes to light when we suddenly realize we have "nothing to do," "nowhere to go," "no one talk to." We now realize *Angst*, a dread which is the complement of our being subjects in the world of objects. It is the dizziness of freedom gazing into its own limitations. (Kierkeggard)

Knowledge

This *Angst* and uncertainty even pervades the world of man's knowledge. The human condition demands that it be interspersed with skepticism. As Ortega y Gasset put it, "The intellectual vigor of a man, like that of a science, is measured by the dose of skepticism and doubt which he is capable of digesting and assimilating."[6] If we are afraid of encountering skepticism and error, we are also fearsome of encountering knowledge and truth.

In our quest for truth, we experience anguish in the realization that we will always be conditioned by the legacy of our parochial culture, as well as by our genes and chromosomes. Although truth may be an absolute, our participation in it will necessarily be finite, relative and historical. This means that in a certain sense, man *is the* measure of all things. This burden makes his an awesome responsibility. It is awesome for this responsibility is not so much to others (that is quite bearable); rather it is a responsibility to oneself (and that is quite overpowering).[7] We dread this and the "object nature" within us would run from it, but we cannot escape this condition of man.

It is man, then, who knows, and what he knows is not an "objective world out there," but a world which can never be free of the coloring and prejudices man gives to it, living as he does in a particular culture, a particular moment of time, and constituted in his physical makeup as he is. (Quite literally, were the eyes of man like those of a fish or an electron microscope, or his ears like those of a dog or giraffe, he would see and hear differently). In short, to talk about "the objective" without any reference to the subject is sheer nonsense. Fortunately, situation ethics can be credited with giving the lie to this sophistry of a "spectator world" and grasping this most fundamental of all facts. The "objective world" as seen through the eyes of a spectator, rather than a participant, is not man's existential world. It must give way to a world having existential priority, to the *Lebenswelt,* the lived world, the homo-relational world, in which time, place, reality all have a man-related—a person-related meaning. *For with man, the personal entered the world and all meaning took on new form.* For all existential meaning is personal, "meaning" being taken here as an "intending."

To illustrate: an engagement ring *means more than what it is* when a young man gives it to a young lady, as opposed to that ring on display in a jewelry shop; a college yearbook *means more than what it is* when dwelled upon by a graduating senior, as opposed to a stranger leafing through it; a toy doll *means more than what it is* in the arms of a little girl at Christmas, as opposed to that doll on exhibit in a store booth.

A spectator view must be transcended by existential man, then, but not only with respect to the world of things; this also applies to the world of men. For it is not only things, but other men who must have a "man-related" meaning. We will see this shortly in our consideration of friendship.

If these views on knowing destroy the world of abstract universals and absolutes, the existentialist says, so be it! We live and die as concrete singulars. Yet we need not exaggerate. The message, that in his own way man makes and creates values and meaning, is clear when we reflect on the commonplace that it is the person who makes a "house a home."

In the language of the phenomenologist, Max Scheler, man is *Weltoffen*—open to the world. Yet even in this, his finitude is revealed by the limit situations (*Grenzsituationen*) which accompany that givenness. These limit situations restrict the deployment of his actions. Their qualities as barriers, sometimes insurmountable, are cyphers reminding us that we ourselves are limited. Examples of these limit situations are: being born in a particular time and culture, knowing that we can never choose with full knowledge, that we must die, etc. Gestalt psychology and depth psychology have been useful in pointing out these characteristics of man's presence in the world.

Friendship

Because man is "world-open," he should not be isolated. His world especially should be the world of friends and his experiences should begin as Buber says, not from the "I am," but from the "we are." This "we" is fundamentally an "I-

Thou" relationship and our attitude to others should be exhibited by a "concern for" rather than the "use of."[8]

To place man in the category of that which is for "my use" is to relegate him to the lesser world of objects.[9] This is what frequently results from a body/soul dichotomy of man, a view that doesn't really see man the person. Perhaps it is also why in times when such a vision of man prevailed, arguments for natural slavery could abound.

If we see the other as a "Thou," an *alter ego*, the body of other could never be an "it," to be sold into economic and hedonistic slavery. Purity would never become a Jansenistic insensitivity to sex as Von Hildebrand rightly observes.[10]

Of course, not all existentialists share this view of man's relationship to other men. Sartre, for example, explicitly declares that "Hell is other people." Yet his vision of man is distorted by his atheism which itself is the logical outcome of his theory of knowledge. That theory is well described by Marcel as a dragnet technique—one that sees each man trying to capture every other man. This is the only way Sartre sees it possible to retain one's own subjectivity—by forcing all others to become objects in my gaze.

None the less, it is true that at times each of us may be the other's hell; however it is also the case that each of us may be the other's heaven. Both are possible precisely because we are persons. Yet Sartre seems too one sided by insisting that every confrontation with others— every *challenge* is a *threat*, instead of an opportunity for mutual growth. Yet, Sartre has exposed a gut issue. Often we do feel uneasy in the presence of another and at such times hide behind the "persona" the mask of the role we play, whether that of a waiter, a professor, a business executive or a bishop. The authentic call of our being is always to shed this mask, this anonymity of the masses in which we fade from our real person.

A revelation of what it is to be a person appears best in

the nature of friendship, then. It is here as Saint Exupery's *Little Prince* shows, that all things take on existential meaning. The fox is explaining to little Prince the nature of friendship as a "taming" of each other. Says the fox,

> But if you tame, it will be as if the sun came to shine on my life. I shall know the sound of a step that will be different from all the others. Other steps send me hurrying back underneath the ground. Yours will call me, like music, out of my burrow. And then look: you see the grain-fields down yonder? I do not eat bread. Wheat is of no use to me. The wheat fields have nothing to say to me. And that is sad. But you have hair that is the color of gold. Think how wonderful that will be when you have tamed me! The grain, which is also golden, will bring me back the thought of you. And I shall love to listen to the wind in the wheat. . . .[11]

Yet friendship is a "letting-be-what-is." It is not a pushy acquaintanceship sought for profit. That is why friendship never discloses nor fully uncovers the "who" of the other. Instead it lets the other reveal himself to me, for eventually, friends wear no masks. This *aletheia* is unlike shame which is someone revealing me when I choose not to be revealed.[12] The bonds of true friendship can never be broken. As Marcel points out, mourning reveals the strength of these bonds, even in death, and so points to the reality of immortality.

Death

This brings us finally to a consideration of the existential meaning of death. Most of us generally avoid any direct reference to the harshness of the reality of death through the euphemisms of "passing away," or "falling asleep." Even when addressing ourselves to the problem, we tend to falsify that which should be our life's concern. Observes Marcel,[13] death is not to be construed as an event, as something that happens, for this is to speak of it with reference to objects, not subjects. The same holds for the view of survival as the "bypassing" of others who have died. Life is not survival and death is not something for the future; rather it is a possibility in and of the present. Of all universal phenomena, death is the most especially my own. And this is why each of us must die his death alone. As Camus puts it, "Death is solitary, whereas slavery is collective."[14]

One cannot remove the dread from death, for both are existential facts of life. As Karl Jaspers says, "Doctors try and talk the sick or those who believe themselves sick out of the fear of death. But these institutions function effectively only when things are going well with the individual. The life-order cannot dispel the dread which is part of every individual's lot."[15] To view death as in the phrase, "Every one has to die sometime," is to see death inauthentically. That such is our normal view is born out by the fact that when death occurs in large numbers, such as in a plane crash, we are always horrified. But if only one passenger dies in such a crash, we pay scant attention to it. Clearly, it is the spectacular and the quantitative that interests us, not the meaning nor even the fact of death.

Some existentialists see death as constituting the unnature of man, as an overcoming of man by his very nothingness. If death is the end of it all, perhaps Sartre is right in claiming man is a "useless passion." But an examination of man reveals there the quality of hope and hope bespeaks immortality. The argument is not to be silenced by an appeal to the purely psychological, for the psychological itself needs for its validation, an ontological base. Death, then, constitutes the existential question of life. Though we are unable to give a final answer to it, we must remain open to its possibilities; and this is to maintain an existential posture toward the mystery of death. More than this, we cannot do.

The Existential Person

Person, then, in an existential perspective, is not to be defined as a "rational supposit" (Boethius) nor an "animal that has reason" (Scholasticism). These definitions fail in part because they are non-relational. More appropriate is the description of person that retains a sense of openness about it. Marcel's "a being who can make promises" is an example, or "he who can always become more than what he is." These suggest ever new horizons on the shifting locus which man reveals his being.

Because of existentialism's view of man as person, it refuses to accept those institutions which treat *man* as a thing, *justice* as a technique, and *love* as essentially calculative and a thing to be measured out. It insists that instinct and reason both be given a place in man's life.[16] Man's person, man's life doesn't find its meaning in an extensional longevity, but always and only in the moment of facing the truth. Because man is person, his philosophy must always be a philosophy of confrontation, of man with the world, of man with life, but primarily of man with himself and other men.

Because man's existence is empirical, contingent and centered around freedom, an existential view of man refuses to place him under the strictures of the a priori, whether these be of behavioristic psychology or ecclesiastical politics. Here again is Sartre's rightful protest about the God of a (decadent) scholastic philosophy—a God who has preconceived blueprints of his creatures to which they *must* conform. Such a

God, in whom all things are somehow predestined, makes it difficult to uphold the characteristic mark of man as person—his freedom. Try as they might, the explainers and apologists of the mystery of predestination seem hellbent on making of man's freedom an unfreedom—of taking away from man so that God might be extolled.

Qualified, in a philosophy of existentialist humanism, there is a measure of truth in Feuerbach's remark that true theology is anthropology. To some extent, the existentialist approach de-emphasizes the attempt to make God anthropomorphic and concentrates instead on making man more theomorphic. Perhaps this too is what Bonhoeffer and some of the "radical theologians" are suggesting. (Of course we might add the rejoinder that Sartre's rejection of such a God does not necessitate the rejection of the God of religion. There is a *marvelous* difference between the God of philosophy and the God of religion—a difference that is entirely existential.[17]

Some Closing Questions

Before concluding, it might be profitable to anticipate some questions about an existential view of man. For example, "Isn't the rejection of reason (which seems implicit in existentialism) the rejection of freedom, and so of the cornerstone of existential man?" If such a rejection were the rejection of all reason, the answer is clearly yes. But the sometimes rejection of reason in existentialism is the rejection of only one kind of reason—Greco-Roman categorical abstract reason—posing in a counterfeit and unauthorized role as a representative of all reasons. There is also Pascal's *logique du coeur* and the reality of connatural knowledge and of affective knowledge. These are hinted at in Aquinas, experienced in mystics and elaborated in Saint Exupery. As the fox of the *Little Prince* says, "It is only with the heart that one can see rightly; what is essential is invisible to the eye."[18]

Another query that might be posed is whether the humanism of an existential view of man is compatible with Christianity. If one sees Christianity as a philosophy, as an ideology, as a system where the Greek *logos* has replaced the Christian *Logos*, the answer is yes, they are incompatible. But if one understands Christianity as a religion, the humanism of existentialism can be said to derive its legacy from the suffering Job, the struggling Augustine and the concerned Francis of Assisi. Well might it be a branch on the trunk of Christian personalism.

In religious experience, for example, faith is always an existential act of the whole man, not just of his intellect. This is why Kierkegaard calls faith an infinite passion. What intelligibility is present in faith is there through love; that is why to the non-lover, faith as well as love make no sense. But then the non-lover is a non-Christian! Person is at the heart of faith. Reflects Marcel, "to believe that . . . I must first believe in," and that in which I believe is always the person who has given witness to faith. Faith then does not reveal objects, but *only the subject*, but it is the subject both of the believer and the one in whom he believes. Because faith has not to do with objects, it is primarily love-promoting, rather than knowledge-yielding. This is why our concern should not be about apologetics, about a worry of losing or keeping the Faith; our concern must be with living the Faith, for in living it, we are loving it, as the etymology of life, love and belief signify.

Our calling as men, as persons, and, especially, as Christians is to see all men existentially, which is to see them as brothers. Here, "to see," means *to bear witness* to the dignity of life. If we "see" men in such a light, we will "see" the existentialist vision of man. It matters not if we understand it; what is important is that we "stand-under" it—that we support the person of all men. That I believe is the message of existentialism—that is its vision of man as person.

Footnotes

[1] Until Christianity began to rid itself of this Platonic view of man as soul, it could not begin to interest itself in man as *in-der-Weltsein*, of man in his dwelling place, the world of space-time. Prior to this moment, the temporal was cast aside as changing and ephemeral. What mattered was not the city of man with its social injustices, but the city of God, where men would meet their equalizer at death.

[2] "Truth is a value and that is why we can love the truth and suffer or die for it." Gabriel Marcel, *Presence and Immortality*, tr. Michael Machado (Pittsburgh: Duquesne University Press, 1968), p. 155. See also Soren Kierkegaard who says, "To grasp truth in a wholly objective fashion is to *eo ipso* remain outside of it." In *Concluding Scientific Postscript*, tr. David Swenson (Princeton: Princeton University Press, 1944).

[3] Cf. Kierkegaard, *Ibid.*, p. 113.

[4] One of the many ways to be guilty of bad faith is to allow the Institution to assume all responsibility for myself, while I agree to serve it without question.

[5] "A faith that celebrates its own triumph is the most ridiculous thing conceivable." Soren Kirkegaard, *Philosophical Fragments*, tr. David Swenson (Princeton: Princeton University Press, 1936), p. 91. Cf. also *The Journals of Soren Kierkegaard*, ed. and tr. Alexander Dru (London Oxford University Press, 1938), #813, p. 261. "The problem is not to understand Christianity but to understand that it cannot be understood."

[6] José Ortega y Gasset, *What is Philosophy?*, tr. Mildred Adams (New York: W. W. Norton Company, Inc., 1960), pp. 51-52.

[7] Joseph Conrad's intriguing novel, *Lord Jim* (New York: Modern Library, 1931), develops this theme. Conrad is clearly in the tradition of existential literature.

[8] Immanuel Kant caught sight of this when he argued that man belongs to the "kingdom of ends."

[9] For a further analysis, see Karl Stern's *The Third Revolution* (New York: Harcourt, Brace & World, Inc., 1955), and Eric Fromm's *The Art of Loving* (New York: Bantam Books, Inc., c. 1956).

[10] This gradual realization of the other as a thou who helps me discover

myself as a person is well illustrated in Miguel de Unamuno's *Nothing Less Than a Man*, in *Three Exemplary Novels*, tr. Angel Flores (New York: Grove Press, Inc. c. 1930), pp. 135-228. In the novel, Alejandro starts out as an abstract ego, a self-made man who adores his maker. But through his wife, Julia, whom he sought as a slave, he becomes a man, a person. At the end, he realizes his mistake of trying to find his fulfillment as a man in terms of power and in terms only of himself.

[11] Antoine de Saint Exupery, *The Little Prince*, tr. Katherine Woods (New York: Harcourt, Brace & World, Inc., c. 1943), p. 83.

[12] For an existential discussion of this and similar themes, see the remarkable book by Alphonsus Jansen. *The Meaning of Love and Marriage*, tr. Geoffrey Stevens and Barbara Waldstein (Techny, Illinois: Divine Word Publications, n.d.).

[13] This is a recurring theme in Marcel's *Presence and Immortality*.

[14] Albert Camus, *The Fall*, tr. Justin O'Brien (New York Vintage Books, c. 1956), p. 136.

[15] Karl Jaspers, *Man in the Modern Age*, tr. Eden and Cedar Paul (Garden City: Doubleday & Company, Inc., 1967), p. 42.

[16] Cf. Dom Aelrad Graham who says, "There is more to be said than is often allowed for trusting one's instincts; they can on occasion prove a safer guide to appropriate action than the careful calculations of reason. Living in a continuous present, one need not be anxious about tomorrow." *Zen Catholicism* (New York: Harcourt, Brace & World, Inc., 1963), p. 155.

[17] For a discussion of this difference, see Jean Danielou's *God and the Ways of Knowing*, tr. Walter Roberts (Cleveland: World Publishing Company, c. 1957).

[18] Saint Exupery, *Ibid.*, p. 87.

THE NEW MARXISM AND HUMAN VALUES

Richard T. De George

In late August, 1968, Soviet troops, accompanied by troops from other East European countries, marched into Czechoslovakia. They were received by the Czechs bitterly, though without violence. The reaction of Americans, as of many in Western Europe, to the Soviet action was generally one of moral indignation.

What I propose to do in this paper is to take this situation as a case study in what might be called international morality. As a part of my analysis I shall establish the categories and structure for a comparative analysis of moralities; I shall conclude by raising the question of the possibility of a truly universal human morality.

If we turn first to the Soviet Union, we can focus our attention on the moral justification which was given for the troop movement (in their view it was not an invasion). There may have been, and undoubtedly were, military, economic, political, and other reasons for the action; but the primary justification which emerged was in terms of morality, and it is with this aspect alone that I am presently concerned. The justification was coolly and cynically received by many in the West. But it was all of a piece with the moral doctrine which had been developing for a long time in the Soviet Union and which had received formalization and increased attention at least since 1956 and more especially since 1961.[1] In brief, the basic moral dictum which forms the basis of Soviet official morality is taken from Lenin, who adapted it from Nechaev: Whatever helps achieve communism is moral, whatever hinders communism is immoral. The basic position is that communism—a state of society in which there is no exploitation, no oppresion, no class division, in which each man has the opportunity to develop fully and freely, in which each will receive what he needs and give what he can—is the moral end of mankind. It is what supposedly all men, whether they realize it explicitly or not, desire. It is a goal which they not only all desire, but which it is right and fitting for them to desire. Add to this moral goal the claim that the Communist Party of the Soviet Union is in the vanguard of those leading mankind to the achievement of its moral destiny, and we have the framework for the moral justification of the occupation of Czechoslovakia: events in Czechoslovakia were threatening the development of socialism not only in Czechoslovakia but also in other countries of Eastern Europe, and could not be properly controlled by the leaders in power. What was happening was thus a threat to the achievement of communism, and hence immoral. It was therefore the international moral duty of the Soviet Union and of other socialist states to intervene to protect what had been achieved. Not only was this specific action justified, but the Party promulgated the international moral duty of socialist states to intervene in the future when the development of communism is threatened.[2]

My purpose here is not to play the jurist and ask whether this doctrine is fully justified within the Soviet scheme, though I believe it is; it is not to ask whether the Soviet scheme itself is justifiable, though I believe it is not; and it is not to ask whether this doctrine can be used by Czechoslovakia or Yugoslavia against developments in the Soviet Union, when and if they believe that the development of communism is being threatened by a return for instance, to Stalinism, though I believe that neither country is capable of such interference, and that the doctrine is practicable only for those who are militarily superior to those who are to be corrected.

The point I would like to emphasize is that in its promulgation of this new moral norm the leaders of the Soviet Union gave a moral justification for their action. In so doing they were acting not unlike the leaders of other nations. The United States's participation in the Vietnamese war is given moral justification by those who defend the Administration position, and both the Arabs and the Israelis give moral justifications for their actions. I have never heard of a country claiming that its military action was anything but moral, and unless it did so it is unlikely that any country could hope to maintain popular support at home or to win at least some respect abroad.

Consequently, what we have in all such instances is a phenomenon which we can call official morality. This is the moral line taken by leaders of nations in defense of their action. This line, moreover, is usually tied in with a number of other officially held and promulgated moral views, which together make up the official morality of a nation. In the case of the Soviet Union, the Party in 1961 proclaimed the Moral Code of the Builder of Communism—a list of twelve moral principles, which were publicized and taught to the people of the Soviet Union by every propaganda device imaginable.[3] Its first principle calls for devotion to the communist cause, and other principles require conscientious labor for the good of society, concern for public property, and collectivism. In the United States the government has never issued a moral code; but it too champions certain values and ideals, and imposes a certain morality on its employees and to a lesser extent on its members through its laws, its spokesmen, and its propaganda. The same is true of other nations.

It is not only possible, but also useful to speak of an official morality, namely that morality which is championed and taught either explicitly or implicitly by the leaders of a country. This morality is very often embodied in the laws of the country. It emerges in the rhetoric of defenses of public actions and programs, and it may include the values and aspirations either held by the people of a nation or seen as necessary for them to hold if they are to achieve certain other goals towards which they aspire. Industrial life requires virtues different from life in an agricultural society. The French revolution gave voice to the cry for Liberty, Equality and Fraternity; the American Revolution gave voice to a desire for men to govern themselves through representatives, and to certain inalienable rights; the Russian Revolution gave voice to the hope for a classless society, free from private property and from the alienation and exploitation which supposedly accompanies it.

Official morality, in the sense in which I have been using it here, is equatable with moral ideology. An ideology is a means by which a people collectively both partially understand and partially misunderstand themselves. It is a way in which a society collectively sees itself, expresses some of its common values, and understands and defends its customs and practices. An ideology in general, therefore, serves a positive function. It goes beyond what constitutes knowledge for an age; it totalizes and sometimes rationalizes the community's experience and institutions. It is a means by which a people can be motivated to join in collective endeavors and work towards common ends, be they the war on poverty, the beautification of highways, the realization of civil rights—or in the Soviet Union the elimination of private ownership of the means of production, the eradication of individualism, or the building of communism. Part of a society's ideology is its public or official morality. The official morality may be imposed from above through propaganda and legal enactment.[4] When this is the case, it might be termed 'manipulative,' though manipulation by moral exhortation or legal enactment need not be morally blameworthy. If, on the other hand, the official morality coincides closely with what the people hold as moral and valuable, it would not be manipulative, but would simply be an expression of the common moral sentiment of a society.

In the case of the movement of Soviet troops into Czechoslovakia and the moral justification given for it, we have an instance of a moral ideology in action. And in the official moral censure given the action by the United States, we have another such instance. Each side claims that its own view is the morally correct one; but each view is based on different premises and a different appraisal of the facts of the case at issue. The official Czech moral stance presents us with a third moral ideology, which coincides with neither of the other two, though it has similarities to both.

I am not here raising the question of how moral ideologies are to be judged better or worse on some objective, independent scale. My purpose now is simply to point out this frequently ignored moral phenomenon. By voicing our indignation over the Soviet action we expressed our moral feelings and gave voice to our moral views. By presenting their justification the Soviets did likewise. That we disagree in our moral evaluation is obvious, though what, if anything, can be done about the disagreement is a question still to be answered.

Official morality or moral ideology is not the only kind of morality that was involved in the Czech situation; nor is it the only kind present in societies. There are two other types or kinds or levels, which we can call 'conformity morality' and 'autonomous morality.'

'Conformity morality' refers to the morality which a people in a society practice and generally live by. It is the morality which arises because of the cultural, social, religious, historical and other factors in a society. It embodies the values generally held and passed on from generation to generation. In a society which is evolving or changing its moral values and views, it is the morality which an individual receives from his peer-group and which is never totally divorced from the other moralities of other groups in the society, if only by the reaction of sons against fathers. Conformity morality is very close to custom and habit. It is the habitual or customary morality which one is taught and with which one grows up. It is the morality which forms the basis for a society's exerting moral pressure against or upon its members. It is not clearly thought out by those who hold it. And those who hold it do so because of training, pressure, habit, fear, or inertia. What I have emphasized is the way this type of morality is held and transferred. I have not mentioned its content. It obviously varies from society to society and from age to age.

Conformity morality is the dominant type of morality in any society. Its content may coincide exactly with a society's moral ideology. But the two are not necessarily identical, nor must they necessarily overlap in even great part. The morality espoused by the Bolsheviks in and after the October revolution did not coincide with the traditional, conformity morality by which many Russians had been living and continued to live after the revolution. The leaders attempted and are still attempting to weed out and do away with what they call the moral remnants of capitalism. The greater the difference between conformity morality and official morality, the more the latter becomes a manipulative morality. The greater the coincidence, the more spontaneous support the leaders have from the people.

'Autonomous morality' is the morality of an individual which he adopts upon reflection and which he adheres to as a personal commitment. It is differentiated from conformity morality not by its content, but by the way it is held. For what one holds after thought, consideration, and personal commitment may coincide with what is generally held by most people from habit and pressure to conform, though it need not so coincide.

If we now turn back to the Soviet-Czech situation we can

analyze it in terms of official, conformity, and autonomous morality. Our analysis will yield nine different moral approaches, namely the official, conformity, and autonomous morality displayed by and in the Soviet Union, Czechoslovakia, and the United States. We have already stated the official moral justification of their action given by the Soviet leaders. To what extent was their view accepted by or to what extent did the Soviet people agree with this view (whether or not they were manipulated into doing so is beside the point)? The indirect evidence we have confirms the claim that the official position was accepted by the Soviet people. There were a number of intellectuals who did not accept the official view, and who protested it in moral terms. The dissidents received a great deal of publicity in the West, partially because they agreed with what many in the West maintained and with the official moral sentiment being expressed there. The Soviet dissidents—or at least some of them—in voicing their moral protest were giving vent to what I have called their autonomous morality. Their moral views were not what was officially held, nor what was generally held by the people of the Soviet Union to be the proper moral response. The dissidents were brought to trial. They expected that their fellow citizens would look upon them as traitors, and as immoral; and they were not disappointed in their expectation. Thus the mass of the Soviet people in their moral reaction and moral views agreed with the official position, while a few did not. There is no way of telling how many in either the majority or the minority position had really thought through their stance and were indeed expressing an autonomous moral judgment and commitment. But at least some of those dissenting must have been doing so.

If the Czech official morality can be equated with the statements of Dubcek and his associates prior to the events of late August, the dissimilarities with the Soviet view of what is moral were noteworthy. Though he agreed that what helps produce communism is moral, he had a quite dissimilar view of what helped produce it, viz., absence of censorship, room for individual initiative, experimentation and change on many levels, national autonomy, and so on. His view did not differ from the Soviet view on ultimate ends, though it did differ on the means which should be adopted and on the evaluation of certain facts, e.g., whether things were getting out of hand, and whether socialism was being threatened. From the spontaneous and electrifying response which this official moral ideology received from the Czech people from January through August, it is clear that it represented their views, gave voice to their feelings and desires, and answered their needs. It expressed the values they actually held, and to this extent the official ideology coincided with the Czech conformity morality. That in many cases it also coincided with the autonomous morality of many is demonstrated by the sacrifices so many Czches made and have been making as individuals, obviously demonstrating a personal commitment to those values. The new ideology which is now being preached at the insistence of the Soviets is clearly manipulative. It is an attempt to present a rationale, a program, a means of understanding their situation which would render the Czech people docile and manageable; and it is clear that its manipulative success is thus far minimal.

The official moral indignation of the United States gave voice to official moral feelings. It should have been no less than it was, if it represents a true moral stance. But it is naive to think that these feelings are the only true and worthy ones, and that any moral person must see things in the way the United States did and does. In the Soviet-Czech case it seems that the official U.S. moral posture coincided with conventional U.S. morality, and was accepted almost without exception by the people of the U.S. Since the voicing of dissent on other issues is evidence that autonomous moral views are often heard in the U.S., there is indirect evidence that the official moral ideology, conventional morality, and autonomous morality pretty well coincided in this instance.

Now on the basis of this preliminary analysis, I should like to briefly do three things: 1) ask what the proper relation among the three types of morality in a society should be; 2) map the differences and similarities among some of the nine moral views I have distinguished; and 3) discuss what could be meant by a universal human morality and whether it is an intelligible and feasible end to attempt to achieve.

1) What the proper relation among official morality, conformity morality, and autonomous morality should be is a complicated question, and the answer to it depends in part on what one believes morality to be.

In the Soviet view, what I have called autonomous morality is not considered a kind of morality at all, if the content of that morality differs from the content of the official morality. The Soviet ethical position claims that there is only one objectively right set of values. These are based on man's needs, they have been nurtured by the working class (which has always represented the bulk of humanity), and they have found their articulation in the writings of Marx, Engels, and Lenin, and in the leadership and pronouncements of the Communist Party of the Soviet Union. What the Party pronounces is objectively valuable, good, and right, and consequently it should be the basis for a correctly formed conscience. The moral values so derived should be collectively held by the members of society, who should help each other embody them. Official morality should be the norm to which conformity morality conforms, and any individual who wishes to be moral should in turn interiorize these norms so that they become his own. If conformity morality does not coincide with the official morality, it should be made to so coincide by legislating the official morality and using official sanctions until social habits, customs and views are reformed. An individual who acts contrary to the values and norms of official morality is not to be respected for his views, but is to be reeducated because his views are mistaken.

This view is consistent if one admits that there is one moral end of mankind, that it entails a commitment individually and collectively to a certain set of values, that the Communist Party of the Soviet Union—for some reason—knows best what these values are, and that in any difference of opinion its view is correct. For if what is objectively right is knowable and known, then each moral person has the obligation to inform himself of what is right and do his best to act in accordance with this knowledge.

If however one doubts that there is only one moral end for mankind, or that there is only one set of objectively valid moral principles or values, or that these are completely knowable or known, or that there is any one group—be it the CPSU or any other—which has privileged access to this knowledge, then the position topples. There is in fact good reason to doubt each of the above claims, the Stalinist reign of terror being the clearest evidence, even for many Soviets, that the CPSU can err in moral matters, and that others can sometimes see objective norms and values more clearly than the Party leadership.

In a pluralistic society there are a variety of ends which members or groups set up for themselves as the proximate moral ends to be achieved, there are a variety of views about what is objectively right, and there are no groups or individuals who can substantiate a claim to infallible moral insight so as to convince all.

In such a situation autonomous morality has historically been taken by philosophers and moralists to be the paradigm case of what morality means. It consists of an individual and personal commitment to values and principles which one has chosen. Here the distinction between an action being right objectively or subjectively becomes important. For to the extent that an individual's conscience is his proximate guide, if he is to be true to himself, he must follow where his conscience leads. An action is thus subjectively valuable from the moral point of view if it is motivated by his sincere convictions and if he acts upon them. He has the obligation to try to justify his convictions and rectify them if they are erroneous by some objective standard he recognizes. But the worth of the moral act consists at least in part in his acting on his convictions. Society has the right to defend itself if it considers his actions contrary to its safety and welfare; but many of the heroes and saints who are recognized in Western history—Antigone, Socrates, Christ—have autonomously held a personal morality which was in some ways at odds with both the conformity and the official morality of their times.

In the absence of infallible objective norms, then, I would argue that a society, if it wishes to maximize the moral value present in the society, both objectively and subjectively, should allow the maximum individuality in moral matters consistent with its reasonable safety and preservation. The means of moral pressure and moral education utilized by such a society should allow for genuine differences of view and should attempt to foster autonomous adherence to values conscientiously embraced, rather than simple conformity. If the divergence among its members is too strong, social cohesion and joint effort may suffer. However, adapting the arguments of John Stuart Mill in *On Liberty*, it is only by the free clash of values that they can be tested and the best ones become recognized; to preclude such clashes is to preclude the unearthing of higher values and ends than those presently held. Social order is not necessarily the highest value which must be bought at the price of severely restricted human freedom. And practically speaking, if the history of mankind thus far is an accurate guide, it is unlikely that very many individuals will be willing or able to search out and live their own autonomously developed values in the face of custom, law, and social inertia. A society composed of automatons who automatically follow what is considered an objectively right line of conduct, would be, so far as subjective moral worth is concerned, a morally empty society.

Whether conformity morality should be legislated or whether conformity morality should be nudged in certain directions by legislation is an issue that has received a good deal of discussion in Western philosophical and legal literature, and it is an issue which I cannot attempt to decide here. It seems to me, however, that the U.S. civil rights legislation was salutary, as has been the civil rights movement which has attempted to bring such legislation up to the moral intuitions of many citizens. In this instance it seems both law and morality have reciprocally aided each other's development.

I feel no compunction about making the hard core racist conform by law to certain values generally and widely held in our society, though even here I must refrain from judging his subjective moral state or value.

2) If we now turn to an overview of the differences and similarities among the various moral views, ideals, and values of the nine moralities we mentioned earlier, we find some overlap among all of them. In the space available here I cannot list all the variants, though a complete map would show where the overlap is in detail. What I shall do is generalize and compare essentially the official Soviet morality as promulgated by the Party and its writers, the official morality which was at least in part enunciated by the leaders of Czechoslovakia before the events of August, 1968, and what I take to be some generally held moral norms and values in the United States.

Marxist doctrine embodies a number of values, and Marxism interpreted in certain ways yields a number of other values. Thus Marx emphasized the moral worth of the freedom of man to develop as a full person and to express himself in a variety of ways. He was opposed to oppression of one man by another, he was opposed to the alienation of man from other men, from the products of his labor, and from the labor process. He saw classlessness as a value. He realized, however, that man's needs could not be taken care of unless society produced sufficient goods through well-developed means of production.

The definition of communism given in the 1961 Party Program is as complete as any, and lists the components of the communist moral ideal: a classless social system, one form of public ownership of the means of production, full social equality for all, all-round development of persons, self-government by free socially conscious workers who give according to their ability and receive according to their need. The Program continues: "A high degree of communist consciousness, industry, discipline, and devotion to the public interest are qualities typifying the man of communist society."[5] To this a few principles can be added from the moral code, also contained in the Party Program. The code spelled out the values which each Soviet citizen was to promote and which he was to see that his fellow citizens promoted as well. Besides devotion to communism, we have: love of socialist countries, conscientious labor for the good of society, concern for public wealth, a sense of public duty, collectivism, mutual respect between individuals, honesty and truthfulness, respect in the family, an uncompromising attitude to injustice, parasitism, dishonesty, careerism, and money-grubbing, intolerance of national and racial hatred, and uncompromising attitude towards the enemies of communism and peace, and solidarity with workingmen everywhere.[6] Not officially listed, though important in the eyes of the Party, and evident to anyone traveling through the Soviet Union is emphasis on those qualities which are essential to production, e.g., punctuality, efficiency, alertness, and so on. The difficulty of getting an agrarian people into the habit of punctuality should not be overlooked, nor the necessity of punctuality for a complex modern industrial plant.

If we compare these values with those officially held by the Czechs, we find a good deal of similarity. Like the Soviets, the Czechs were devoted to socialism in the present and to communism as an ultimate goal to be achieved. They promoted those virtues and traits necessary for industrial production. But where we find differences is in the interpretation and approach to such terms as 'freedom.' For the Czechs wished to implement freedom of discussion and freedom from censorship to a degree not tolerated by the leaders of the Soviet Union. They favored attempts at letting the workers have more of a voice in their own affairs, including productive affairs. They were willing to let the Party have less of an iron hand over the lives of the people so that the people could develop themselves more fully and completely at the present time, and prepare themselves for the gradual withering away of the state and the achievement of self-government.

The official Czech morality, at least nominally, did not violently disagree with that enunciated by the Soviets. But it did call for an implementation of the humanistic principles contained in Marxism sooner than the Soviets were willing to allow, and it did allow for a lessening of the role of the Communist Party in the complete direction of the affairs of the country. The first point to note is that there was no desire or tendency on the part of the official ideologues—nor on the part of most Czechs—to choose capitalism over communism. They accepted Marx's critique of capitalism, they wished to avoid its evils, and they wished to attain the good life Marx described. They moreover agreed with the Soviet conception of what that good life would ultimately consist of. Here the overlap with the Soviet moral view is considerable. They disagreed, however, with the Soviets on the means to achieve the goal of communism and the rate at which certain values which both they and the Soviets espouse—at least verbally—should be implemented.

If we now introduce the U.S. scheme of values, it is clear that at least in those areas where certain values or virtues or qualities are necessary for industrial production, there are areas of overlap. It is also interesting that most of the values contained in the statement of communism are values which most Americans would feel are worthwhile—freedom, all-round development of the person, cultural and educational opportunities, absence of oppression and alienation, absence of poverty with each man having what he needs and each contributing what he can. Freedom of speech and lack of censorship are values which the Czechs had espoused in a way which endeared them to the heart of most Americans, to an extent comparable to the fear it raised in the hearts of the Soviet leaders. National autonomy and political self-determination are also values which the Czechs opted for and which overlapped with values the U.S. officially champions, in opposition to the Russian position.

The Czech position can thus be seen to fall somewhere between the U.S. and Soviet positions, though it overlaps more with the Soviet moral ideology, and though all three moral ideologies overlap to some extent.

Because of the many attempts at Christian-Marxist dialogues, existentialist-Marxist dialogues, and the like, I should like to point out i) that there are some real instances of genuine overlap in the values held, and that consequently some ground exists for common ventures and for action towards similar limited goals; ii) there are some instances where the different ideologies use the same terms, but in fact mean different things by these terms. One instance, as we have seen, is in the use of the word 'freedom'; iii) there are times when both sides agree on ends and terms, but disagree on the facts of a question; and iv) there are times when there is genuine difference on what is valuable. I shall say a word about each of the four cases.

i) Where there is genuine overlap in the values held, we may find ground for joint action. These might be cases where the enlightened self-interest of both sides is operative. The official Soviet desire for promoting peace, where this means the absence of nuclear war, coincides with the U.S. desire to promote peace in the same sense, and lays the ground for certain contacts, meetings, and at lest some cooperation. The non-proliferation of nuclear bombs and the banning of atomic testing above the surface (lest excessive fallout and contamination result) are other areas of cooperation. On lower echelons, in some countries of both Eastern and Western Europe, communists have joined with members of other parties and groups for specific humanitarian, social welfare, and other projects.

ii) Those instances where two or more moral ideals are expressed in the same language but where different things are meant by them cause much confusion. They lead to charges of insincerity on both sides, and raise hopes which cannot be satisfied. Experience shows that it is easier to agree on some common course of action than on an abstract set of principles, if the principles are to be spelled out. The difference in meaning may come about for a variety of reasons—historical, intellectual, social, or other. The Soviet view of freedom is closely linked with a Marxist-Leninist social theory and with a collectivist view of man. The Soviet claim is that man can only be free when all men are free, and this can only be achieved in a society which has done away with classes, the division of labor, and private property. For most Americans freedom involves the right to choose one's representatives, to travel without restraint, to print and read criticism of the government, and so on. Americans who use this criterion rightly claim that freedom in this sense does not exist in the Soviet Union. Soviets using their meaning of the term rightly claim that freedom does not exist in the United States. It is well to note that each side espouses freedom, but that each side means something at least somewhat different from the other by the term. A complete analysis of the amount of overlap might prove enlightening, though a consciousness of differences is likewise important.

iii) I have already pointed to the Soviet-Czech affair as one instance in which the Czechs and Soviets disagreed on the facts of a case, though they agreed on a number of principles and values. The Soviets claimed that the Czech leadership had lost control of many forces within the country and that consequently socialism was threatened. This description of the state of affairs in Czechoslovakia was denied by the Czech leaders. At stake were also differences of value, e.g., the value of self-determination; but this aside, there was a real difference on the evaluation of facts. The present instance tends towards the conclusion that differences of fact are sometimes adjudicated by might. Where strength is faced with strength there is both the hope of arbitration and the fear of conflagration.

iv) The cases of genuine differences on what is valuable are many. The Soviets claim that private ownership of the means of production is inherently evil; most Americans feel that it is not. The Soviets are opposed to the division of labor, which to many Americans seems not necessarily evil; the Soviets condemn classes and class divisions, which do not appear inherently evil to many Americans. Many Americans, on the other hand, would defend the moral right of an artist to create what he chooses and would condemn Soviet censorship and restraint on artists, their imprisonment for parasitism, and the like. The list of differing evaluations could be generated at will.

The differences can in some cases be reduced to differences of belief, and to differences of attitude. Where there are truly differences of belief, there may perhaps be some means of arriving at a decision about which beliefs are correct, though they are often so intertwined with attitudes that this is very difficult. Where there are truly differences of attitude, one may hope that eventually facts and practical states of affairs may alter attitudes and prepare the ground for agreement; but this is a hope which seems destined not to be realized in the near future.

The question of whether man is truly a collective being seems, for instance, to be based in part on factual matters, in part on beliefs and attitudes. It is not at all clear at this time how to show the superiority or truth of either this or of some alternative view. Similarly one's judgment about the morality of private property is not simply a question of fact, but involves beliefs and attitudes. Does private property necessarily lead to oppression? Does its suppression necessarily lead to worse evils, such as were produced in the Soviet Union during its early history? How conflicts on values are to be adjudicated, how attitudes can be changed, and what the psychological relation of values to facts really is, are still areas in which there are no clear answers.

3) This state of affairs leads me to the last of the topics I proposed to treat in this paper. What do we mean by a universal human morality, and what might be the possibility of agreeing on one and achieving it?

The Soviet answer to these questions is simple and straightforward. Communist morality, we are told, is the universal human morality. It embodies and grew out of the simple norms necessary for any society. It was developed by the workers of the world and came to be clarified more and more clearly with time. It was articulated by Marx, Engels, Lenin, and the Communist Party of the Soviet Union. We have already seen the claim that communism is the implicit moral goal of all mankind. The morality which will produce that society and which will be found exemplified therein, governing the relations between man and man, is communist morality. When all mankind is united in communism, then will all mankind be governed by and enjoy the universal human morality.

The Soviet view of what constitutes a universal human morality is not only simple; it is simplistic. It is a monolithic morality for a communistic society in a far distant future. It is closed to any pluralism of moral points of view, since it rests satisfied that its view is true, and that any conflicting view must therefore be false. It is a morality for the new men of communist society, a society which is to be achieved by the weeding out and wiping out of capitalists, the bourgeoisie, nonconformists and others. It is a humanism of the future for the men of the future.

The Soviet solution gives one meaning to 'universal morality' and 'universal moral values'; but the premise of the solution is the existence of a universal communistic society. Does the notion of universal moral values make sense in the present divided, fragmented, pluralistic world with its conflicting and competing values?

The question might be answered in several ways. We might, for instance, (a) equate 'universal morality' with general agreement among the official moralities or moral ideologies of all countries. If it were possible to achieve an international moral order, this might satisfy the requirement of a universal morality. To ask for more might be (b) to ask that the conformity morality of all nations and all peoples should be the same, i.e., that they should all acknowledge the same actions and values as good and the same ones as bad. Or even further, the demand for a universal human morality might be (c) a demand that the official, conformity, and autonomous morality of all nations, of all peoples, and of all persons overlap perfectly.

View (c) is the most ideal of the three. Yet it seems to me it is a false ideal. For it presupposes human uniformity which is not to be found. Either tolerance is a value which would find no place in such a world; or tolerance of diversity would allow for real moral differences. View (c) also implies that values can be found once and for all. Since autonomous and conformity morality must coincide, the view allows no room for the innovator, the creative moral man who forges new ways of acting, who discovers or elevates new moral values not yet sufficiently recognized by his peers.

The Soviet view is, it seems to me, at least partially correct in drawing attention to the simple rules of morality necessary for the continuation of any society. These would include moral rules concerning the taking of life, the regulation of commerce, the fostering of truth-telling, the promoting of trust necessary for social intercourse and cooperation, and the like. These are rules without which a society would not be able to function as a society. They are rules which a society must adopt in some form or other if it is to survive. Now if this is an accurate picture of human societies, then all presently existing societies must have some such simple rules. There is no need for them all to be the same, and there are no difficulties as long as people stay in their own societies. Presumably the moral values and forms in each society will change, develop, or evolve as conditions change or as moral insight grows. But the self-righteous, those who believe they have found the true human morality or the truly universal human values, have no right to impose their views upon any other individual or group. For to do so would be in fact to preclude autonomous morality for those upon whom some outside norms are imposed.

Since in fact, however, human societies are not independent groups, but groups sharing a rapidly shrinking planet, what is needed and what has not yet evolved is the recognition on a worldwide level of simple moral rules and values which all can acknowledge and adhere to for the common purpose of keeping society as such, and the human race as such, alive. Just as early societies needed rules to insure simple survival, so today does the world need to recognize such simple rules. The quest for universal human values should begin with a quest for those values which must be generally acknowledged if mankind is to survive. The particular values which emerge and are agreed upon as necessary may be similar to those which have been adopted on lower levels of social life; but they need not be identical, and the fact that many different sets of moral norms work on the lower levels suggests that there is no one magic formula or set, any more than there is one magic constitution or form of government, or one goal which is envisaged by all men.

It is a mistake to think that there is only one end which all men desire or that the moral ideal is unique, definable, and the same for all men. If happiness be the end of each, it is not clear that it would be the same for all. The difficulties of the opposite view have been sufficiently expounded since the days of Aristotle to need little development here.

The absence of nuclear warfare is one common goal to which at least the United States and the USSR seem committed in principle, but one about which China and countries of the Near East seem still uncertain. The eradication of starvation is a goal to which no major power seems completely dedicated. If on specific goals such as this there seems to be as yet little agreement, how much more idealistic would it be to expect agreement on both the meaning and the application of the concept of social justice on an international level. We have seen that national autonomy, though nominally recognized by the

U.N., in practice is open to the widest interpretation by countries such as the USSR with respect to Czechoslovakia.

If we are to draw any conclusions from all this I suggest the following: 1) Marxism, as developed in the Soviet Union and in other countries of Eastern Europe, provides a framework for a moral ideology. The ideology is very similar from one of these countries to another; though there are differences at least in means and in emphasis from one to another. The degree of overlap of Marxist moral ideology with U.S. moral ideology is not negligible, but is very often more verbal than actual. Cooperation is possible within limits in spite of, rather than because of, these ideological stances. 2) The communist ideal of a universal morality is monolithic in character. Any monolithic morality is inconsistent with the present plurality of moral values and outlooks. 3) A single universal morality on all levels of morality seems neither necessary nor desirable. 4) Where an attempt should be made to reach accord on the practical, if not on the theoretical level, is in the area of international relations, where self-preservation may serve as the basis common to all peoples. A nexus of overlapping and intertwining moral ideologies, with differences on the national level, and even greater differences on the level of autonomous morality seems a more clearly attainable moral community to which mankind might presently aspire, than one in which complete uniformity and moral agreement are demanded.

Moral diversity and freedom to choose from among competing moral values are themselves moral values which should not be too lightly dismissed. Classical Marxism had no room for such a view; Soviet Marxis-Leninism officially has no room for such a view. But the exigencies of practice have wrought changes in Marxist theory in the past. Worldwide demands and the developing humanistic new Marxism, especially as found in non-Soviet Eastern Europe,[7] may yield Marxists who, while not giving up their views, are willing to accommodate to a pluralistic world in which they cooperate with others. No man and no country need or should compromise his values; he need merely see that there is more good on the whole to be gained by not attempting to impose his views on others than by attempting to impose them. The strict Marxist, while admitting other nations to the moral community, can rest content in his belief that eventually his morality will be recognized by all. But every other moral ideologist can dream the same dream. The restraint and willingness to let the supposedly true morality triumph in the only way it can—by being recognized on its own merits—and the corresponding renunciation of any attempt to impose one's values by force, is the *sine qua non* for there being any humans left to be part of a moral human community.

Not all moralities are equally good. But until we can find some objectively agreed upon way of deciding and convincing everyone concerned which is the best morality, the way of prudence lies in accepting the moral least common denominator which will render communal life on a global scale tolerable.

Footnotes

[1] For a detailed presentation of Soviet moral doctrine and its development, see Richard T. De George, *Soviet Ethics and Morality* (Ann Arbor: Michigan University Press, 1969).

[2] See, for instance, the article "Sovereignty and International Duties of Socialist Country," published in *Pravda* (September 25, 1968). A full translation appeared in *The New York Times* (September 27, 1968), p. 3.

[3] Part II, V, (1) of the Party Program. An English translation is contained in *The Road to Communism: Documents of the 22nd Congress of the Communist Party of the Soviet Union* (Moscow: Foreign Languages Publishing House, 1961), pp. 566-567.

⁴ Thus Krushchev could say, "If the moral consciousness of a particular worker is not as high as it should be, then demand by law that he act in the way he should." (This quotation is from a speech delivered on December 14, 1961, and reprinted in part in *Communist Morality* (Moscow: Progress Publishers), p. 194.

⁵ *The Road to Communism*, p. 509.

⁶ Ibid., pp. 566-567.

⁷ For a fuller discussion of these developments, see Richard T. De George, *The New Marxism: Soviet and East European Marxism Since 1956* (New York: Pegasus, 1968).

THE TIME OF OUR LIVES

Mortimer J. Adler

The title of this lecture involves a triple play on words. It means, first of all, the span of time alloted to each of us, the time we use up as we live from day to day, month to month, year to year. Secondly it has this meaning: when we return from a trip—either geographical or psychedelic—we say we had the time of our lives, meaning a good time, a fun time. The third meaning is the time in which our lives are now being lived—this century. This triple play on words is intended. First, because, the basic moral choice that I am going to deal with is the choice between having a good time and leading a good life. And secondly, from the point of view of leading a good life—not having a good time—this is the best century so far to be alive in. You may doubt that, but I am going to try to prove that to you.

This lecture is a condensation of a book of mine, *The Time of our Lives*, published in 1970. There are risks in doing this because of the abbreviations, the things left unclear, and arguments that are not as persuasive as they might be. I ask you to do me the courtesy of believing that in the book there are no short cuts.

Let me give you a little background on the book itself. As I explain in the book's postscript, it consists in a rewriting of Aristotle's *Ethics* for the twentieth century. For 45 years now, and in the light of my knowledge of the whole history of Western thought, I can say without exaggeration, first, that the *Ethics*, written in the 4th century BC, is the only sound, practical, and undogmatic treatise on moral philosophy; second, that since the 15th century, it has not been carefully studied and even when it has been read by modern philosophers, such as John Locke, Kant, J. S. Mill, or John Dewey, it has not been understood by them. In fact, it has been badly misunderstood; and third, that in our century, it is almost totally neglected by philosophers and almost totally neglected in our universities.

This leads me to call your attention to what I find a startling fact, and which you may find so too. That is, that the highest development of human wisdom in the West, especially moral or practical wisdom, occurred in the 5th and 4th century BC. It was preserved and extended a little in subsequent centuries, especially in the 12th and 13th centuries in the great medieval universities. But it has been lost in modern times—progressively from the 17th to the 20th century—and especially in our universities and among our men of learning. Our great gains in science and technology have been accompanied by an almost complete loss of wisdom, though this need not have been the case. The accidents that brought it about, and are still responsible for it today, are the accidents of bad schooling and bad education, together with a juvenile attitude on the part of modern men toward the past. This is the same kind of juvenile attitude that the young today exhibit toward their elders.

As a result, moral philosophy in modern times is a barren waste born of errors and of ignorances that could have been avoided. In place of moral wisdom, we have moral skepticism and moral relativism or, worse, the existentialist despair about the meaninglessness of life. This is a product not only of errors in philosophy, but also of erroneous conclusions drawn from the social sciences, especially comparative and cultural anthropology.

I mention all this to call your attention to an astounding paradox. The dissident and rebellious young, under the influence of their college professors, together with the leaders of the New Left and others who are full of complaints about our century and our society, do not hesitate to make moral pronouncements about the evils they think must be done away with—and they make these pronouncements with a certitude that sounds as if they could defend them on clear moral principles and by the most cogent reasoning.

I would like to read you a brief statement by George Kennan—whom I regard as one of the sanest and most judicious minds in this country—which appeared in the *New York Times*, January 21, 1968. The title of this article is "Rebels Without a Program." Mr. Kennan writes: "What strikes one first about the angry militancy is the extraordinary degree of certainty of one's own rectitude, certainty of the correctness of one's own answers, certainty of the accuracy and profundity of one's own analysis of the problems of contemporary society, certainty as to the iniquity of those who disagree." He then goes on to say: "One is struck to see such massive certainties already present in the minds of people who not only have not studied very much but presumably are not studying a great deal, because it is hard to imagine that the activities to which this aroused portion of our student population gives itself are ones readily compatible with quiet and successful study."

At the same time, it is perfectly clear that those who pass these high moral judgments full of certitude do not know or understand the principles on which their criticisms might be based, and have not engaged in the reasoning which might defend them. On the contrary, they have repudiated these principles and such reasoning. For exactly the same principles that might support criticism of the war in Vietnam, or of racism, or of poverty, or of a society that tends toward overindulgence in play or the over-production of superfluous commodities, exactly the same principles and reasoning would also help them to understand what is wrong with being a beatnik or a hippie—wrong in a way that can ruin a human life; or what is wrong with over-indulgence in sex; what is wrong with psychedelic escapism, with the expansion of the sensual life and the contraction of the mind; with the rejection of reason; and so on. Exactly the same moral principles are involved but they are certain about one and have no moral judgment about the other. I will return to this paradox later.

The fault in the case of the young is not theirs. It is ours. We have failed them educationally. Their minds have not been opened to any wisdom at all, nor trained to seek it. We, in the 20th century, are reaping the fruit whose seeds have been sown from the beginning of the 17th century.

Our final introductory remark: last year in Aspen, I had the pleasant opportunity and occasion to engage with Dr. Wing-Tsit Chan, a noted Chinese scholar, in a joint East-West seminar. The assignment for both of us was a lovely one. He would tell what Confucious' views on the good life for man, and I would report briefly Aristotle's views on the same subject. With few exceptions, really quite remarkable because we had not planned this or prepared it, the same fundamental moral wisdom about what is involved in making a good life appeared in these brief statements of Confucius and of Aristotle. The only difference is that in China the wisdom of Confucius has been preserved and the wisdom of Aristotle has been lost in the West.

I will begin with a brief summary of the basic moral problem and then discuss the solution to it. I am going to start with an initial and imperfect statement of the problem that is expressed in the question: How can I make a good life for myself? We are given a span of time—fifty, sixty, seventy, eighty years. How shall I best use it? A whole life is a succession of days, months, and years filled by activities, or inactivities, of one sort or another. We make that life by our choices from day to day; by how we choose to use or consume our time.

Consider the analogy of making a life with making a building. The insight is very simple from the analogy. Since what happens at the end in the process of building is effected by what happens at the beginning and all along the way, it would be much better, would it not, when one is erecting a building to have a plan of some sort? So perfectly obvious in the case of a building, why is it not equally obvious that if you are building a life, a plan of some sort would help? There is a defect in the analogy, however, because the building is a spatial, not a temporal whole. Hence after you build it you can have it, live in it, enjoy it, look at it. But a life is not a spatial whole; a life is a temporal whole, and you cannot have a whole good life at any moment of time. There is no moment in your life's time when you can enjoy your whole life.

Hence there is a confusion in everybody's mind about the meaning of the word "happiness," for most people use the word happiness for a good time, but I want to use the word happiness not for a good time but for a whole good life. Using it that way, I must say that happiness, like a whole good life, is totally unexperienceable and unenjoyable.

Let me take another analogy—the analogy of the performing arts. Here we find the same fundamental insight. If you are a performing artist, you carry out a plan. The music is part of the plan, but your own handling of the music is also part of the plan. This analogy is better because the performance of a symphony is a temporal whole. Yet this analogy is defective also because the performing artist can engage in one or more rehearsals before he performs, but there is no rehearsal in life. You have to start from scratch.

Nevertheless, with this defect acknowledged, the analogy is instructive because a good performance is good as a whole through being good in its parts and through their order to one another. It cannot be called good as a whole until it is finished. While it is in process, all we can say is that it is *becoming* good. If you were to stop a performance in the middle and ask "Is it good?" the answer should be "No, it is not good yet; it is becoming good." The same is true of a whole human life.

These analogies are helpful, but in one profound respect they are misleading. We are under no moral obligation to make any particular work of art. No categorical moral obligation—unconditional, absolute. If an artist wishes to produce a certain work, he may be under a certain obligation to do as good a job as possible—but only on the condition that he wishes to do so. This is a hypothetical or conditional obligation, not a categorical or moral obligation. There is no morality at all without categorical or unconditional obligations. Furthermore, there is no morality unless these categorical obligations are the same for all men at all times and places. Moral principles are not valid as moral principles unless they are universalizable, applicable to all men as men. Hence the moral problem of making a good life differs fundamentally from the artistic problem of making a good work, or any similar technological problem of producing a good result.

This leads us at once to a transformation of the initial question. It is not "How can I make a good life for myself, if I wish too?" That question might be answered by pragmatic know-how. Rather the question is "What must I do in order to make for myself the good life that I *ought* to make, that I am under a categorical moral obligation to make?"

Now let me clarify the problem as restated. If a temporal whole, like a life, is an ultimate goal, it must be a normative, not a terminal, end. I use the words goal, objective, or end as synonyms. A good life is something you aim at, but as an end it controls the means normatively, not terminally, because you never arrive at it. Chicago may be the terminal end of a railroad trip; it can be arrived at. In this sense death is the terminal end of life. But a good life is not a terminal end. Yet the conception of your whole life operates normatively at every moment of your life to control what you do.

That a good life is an ultimate as well as a normative end is clear from the fact that there is nothing beyond it to which it can possibly serve as a means. No one can complete either one of the following two sentences: "I want to be happy because I want . . ." or "I want a whole good life for the sake of . . ." The sentences are impossible to complete because happiness or a whole good life cannot be a means to anything. They are ultimate ends or objectives. To say that happiness or a whole good life is both an ultimate and normative end is to say that it is the standard or measure for judging the goodness of all the means we employ or the parts we put together to make that whole, the choices we make about the ordering of the parts, and the other factors that enter into the whole process of seeking the goal we are morally obligated to seek.

Since it is a whole constituted of parts, this ultimate, normative end should not be called, as it so often is, the *summum bonum*, but the *totum bonum*. It is not the highest partial good in a scale of partial goods which is what the word *summum bonum* means, but the one and only whole of goods, including all partial goods as its parts, which is what the word *totum bonum* means. A Roman stoic and statesman by the name of Boethius summarizes all this in one sentence: "Happiness consists in a whole life made perfect by the possession in aggregate of all good things"—possession successively in the course of time, not simultaneously, or at one moment. Contrast that with the promise that the devil made to Faust if Faust would sell his soul to the devil in Goethe's play. The words that Faust uses in that little bargain are "I will give you my soul if any moment of my life is so perfect that I am impelled to say 'Stay, thou art so fair!'" That moment never occurs; there is no moment in life to which anyone can say "Stay, thou art so fair!"

Happiness, or the good life, cannot be the ultimate, normative end that we are categorically obligated to seek unless it is the same for all men. This is the hardest thing for most people today to understand. Let me explain it by taking two steps carefully. First, the equality of men as men is true only if all members of the human species have a sameness of specific nature. That is the only meaning that can be attached to the truth that all men are born equal—equal genetically as men, in spite of all their individual differences and inequalities. If this is true, then basic human needs and potentialities are the same for all men at all times and places, regardless of the accidental historic circumstances surrounding individual human lives.

If you understand the specific nature of flowers or dogs, you understand the standards by which, at flower shows or dog shows, the judges award the blue ribbon to the specimen that is entitled to be called not just best of breed but best in show, though the particular flower may be a rose and the particular dog may be a Schnauzer. The same kind of standard can be applied to men, seen in terms of the lives they lead and how their lives bring their natures to bloom or perfection.

The second step may be a little more difficult, but it is absolutely indispensable. This point is the stumbling block of all modern philosophers. It is the distinction between the real and the apparent good. Spinoza asked the following question: Do we call something good simply because we do in fact desire it, or should we, ought we, desire some things because in fact they are good for us? Spinoza chose the first alternative: what is called good is as various as individuals and their actual desires. Applied to happiness, this means that the good life for each man is just what he himself conceives it to be; in terms of the things that he wants for himself. Hence the miser is happy, not miserable. He gets what he wants when he has that pile of gold. There is no objective standard by which we can say to the miser, who is content with his pile of gold, that he is a miserable creature, one who has ruined his own life. This fine theory now goes by the name of "the emotive theory of values."

No one can deny, said Socrates, that all men seek what they deem advantageous or beneficial to themselves. Granted this, can men not make mistakes about what is beneficial or detrimental? Socrates' answer is "Yes, men often make mistakes. They often overeat or overdrink and ruin their health; or they waste their time getting more wealth than they need or can use to their profit, and so on." If Socrates is right, as I think he is, and Spinoza is wrong, then not all things that a man actually desires are really good for him even when they appear to be so, because he has *mistakenly* deemed them to be to his advantage. Contrariwise, a given individual may mistakenly deem to be evil, or actually not desire, things that are really good for him, the lack of which can prevent his life from being a good human life.

For example, the miser, or the power-hungry man, or the man who devotes all his time and efforts to sensual indulgences of one sort or another, has excluded from his life things that are really good for him though he has everything he wants. He can pursue and succeed in getting everything he wants, though most of the things he wants are not good for him in the quantity in which he wants them and gets them.

The basic vocabulary we must use to hold this distinction in mind involves a distinction between natural needs—which may or may not be conscious—and conscious wants, the wants we are conscious of, the desires elicited by our experience and environment. Our conscious wants may or may not represent our natural needs. Natural needs are the same for all men because of their common human nature, but conscious wants differ from individual to individual.

The basic self-evident truth here is that the good is the

desirable; and the desirable, the good. But there are two types of desirables—the desirable that is naturally needed and the desirable that is consciously wanted, whether or not it is naturally needed. Now the desirable that is naturally needed is that which is really good, and really good for each and every man; whereas the desirable that is consciously wanted, differing from man to man, is the apparent good, the thing a man *calls* good because he actually desires it. We are under no obligation to seek apparent goods; they are simply the things we call good because we actually want them. Only with respect to real goods—the things that are good because we need them, whether we want them or not—can it be said that we *ought* to desire them, even when we do not in fact desire them.

In short, the categorical moral obligation "Seek the good" applies only to real goods; it makes no sense in the case of goods that are merely apparent. The categorical moral obligation to make a good life for one's self must be understood as meaning "a really good life." That good life is the same for all men, because the real goods that constitute it are the same for all men.

One more point must be made to assure understanding of the moral problem. If life were a day-to-day affair, we would either have no moral problem at all, or it would be so simple as to deserve little thought. If at the end of day we closed the books, if there were no carry-over of accounts from one day to the next, if what happened to us in the days of our childhood, or if what we did when we were young, had little or no effect on the rest of our lives, then our choices would all be momentary and passing ones. A jug of wine, a loaf of bread, and thou might be enough wisdom for life on a day-to-day basis. In fact, this is the way that animals do live—on a day-to-day basis, without a thought for the morrow, except in the case of certain hoarding instincts which involve no thought on the animal's part.

The problem of making a whole human life that is really good—good in each of its parts, and good in a way that results from each part contributing what it ought to contribute to the whole—exists for us precisely because, at every stage of our lives, in every day of our existence, we are faced with the basic moral alternative—a good time today *versus* a good life as a whole.

The great misfortune of the human race, in every generation, is that its young or immature members—at the time of their lives when it would be most important to understand this—find it extremely *difficult* to understand. That is the essence of youth or immaturity: not understanding the long run *versus* the short run. By this standard, many who are chronologically adult are morally immature; and some few who are chronologically young are morally mature. If it is *merely very difficult, not impossible*, for the chronologically young to understand this, then you can see the importance of sound moral instruction and training to bring them to maturity at the earliest possible date in their lives. The mature man who understands it only too well is often too late to make the best use of this wisdom. Here is our most dismal failure—the failure of our school, our teachers, our parents, our era.

The problem now being understood, what in the most general terms is its solution? The briefest way to indicate the outlines of the solution is by an enumeration of all the real goods that satisfy man's natural needs, and by naming the human activities that we must engage in to procure them.

HEALTH AND VIGOR OF THE BODY	biologically necessary activities, such as sleeping, eating, cleansing, and sometimes playing, when playing is therapeutic or recreational. *SLEEP*

WEALTH or the means of subsistence, the comforts and conveniences of life	economically necessary activities, such as working for a living, or managing one's estate. *SUBSISTENCE-WORK*
PLEASURE in all its experienceable forms, both sensual and aesthetic	all forms of activity engaged in wholly for their own sake, with no result beyond themselves. PLAY (pure play, not therapeutic play.)
FRIENDSHIPS: love and companionships	
A GOOD SOCIETY: external peace, and security with regard to the goods of fortune	all forms of activity by which the individual improves himself and contributes to the improvement of his society: *LEISURE-WORK*
KNOWLEDGE: skills, understanding, wisdom	

Of these six basic types or classes of real goods, the first three represent limited goods—goods that are good only in some limited quantity. Only the last three are unlimited goods—goods of which you can never have enough.

On the four basic types of human activity, only one—the one that corresponds to the three unlimited goods—calls for the maximum investment of our time, and that is leisure-work: the kind of activity by which are individual grows or develops as a human being. The biologically necessary activities are common to men and all other animals. The economically necessary activities, since they provide the conditions of bodily health and vigor, are for the most part on the same level. While purely playful activities are good in themselves, providing us with immediately enjoyable pleasures, they do not increase our human stature one cubit, and so while they are good, they are good only in a limited quantity. Only leisure activities—activities that are creative in the primary sense of being self-creative, not productive of other things—contribute, first of all, to the growth of a human being as specifically human: and secondly, to the improvement of human society and the advancement of human culture.

Hence in the moral choices that we make from day to day in the use of our time, we ought to subordinate all other activities to engagement in leisure-work. We ought to engage in the others only to an extent that is based on real needs—our natural needs—or that is limited by the consideration that nothing that we do should cut into the time that is left free for leisuring.

Since the temptations of a good time, of pleasure in the passing moment, are great; since it is so easy to want more wealth than we need; since it is so easy to shirk or wish to avoid the pains and efforts involved in doing leisure-work, what is required to make the moral choices that we ought to make in order to work for the end that we ought to seek—a whole life that is really good because it involves all the things that are really good for a man, all of them in the right order and proportion? The only answer to this question is moral virtue, which is nothing but a habitual disposition to prefer a good life to a good time, to choose what is really good in the long run over what is apparently good here and now. This is the meaning of "strength of character." This is the meaning of such moral virtues as temperance and fortitude. Along with them go another indispensable virtue: prudence, that is, sound judgment in choosing among particular means, here and now, under all the complicated circumstances of each particular case in which we have to choose.

Unlike all the other means to a good life—the real goods that I have enumerated as constituting it—the virtues are primarily operative or functional, not constitutive means.

In naming the virtues, I have mentioned all the principal ones except justice. This alone of all the virtues concerns the good of other men. I have so far been considering only each man's moral obligation to make a good life for himself. I will come to justice in a moment, when I consider the individual's obligations with respect to other human beings and the good life for each of them.

One point remains to complete this extremely brief sketch of the solution of the moral problem. Some of the real goods we need are wholly or partly in the hands of fortune—are wholly or partly beyond our own control. For example, the kind of parents we have, the kind of home that surrounds our early years, the kind of early schooling we receive, are wholly beyond our own control, yet seriously affect our lives and the choices we are confronted with in later years. Other goods, such as our health, are favorably or adversely affected by the environment, which may be controlled to some extent by the organized community, but not very much by the individual. The state of technology and the organization of the economy effect the character and the amount of subsistence work we are compelled to do, and the amount of free time we have left over from sleep, play, and such subsistence work. The political organization of society and its institutions, along with its basic economy, gives to or withholds from individuals the basic freedoms they need in order to make a good life for themselves. Chattel slaves or the subjects of a despotic government are deprived of essential freedoms.

In short, when I speak of the goods of fortune, I have in mind all these things that enter into an individual's life but over which he does not have complete control, as he does have complete control over the use of such part of his time as is left free from all compulsory activities, biological or economic.

One little story helps to make the point clear. Plutarch tells us that someone once asked Plato in what respects he considered himself blessed by good fortune. His answer was: that I was born a Greek rather than a barbarian, a free man rather than a slave, and in the time of Socrates rather than in some other time. But Plato would have added—though Plutarch does not— that these were blessings only for a man who knew how to use such good fortune in making a really good life for himself.

I must stress this point. It is of great importance in the rest of this lecture. Good fortune only provides the opportunities a man needs; whether he makes a good use of them is entirely a matter of his own choice. Other Athenians shared the same blessings that Plato was grateful for, and many—perhaps most of them—did not use them as he did. Why? Because making a good life for one's self—fulfilling this moral obligation—is the hardest, not the easiest, thing for a man to do. As Spinoza said, whatever is excellent or noble is as difficult as it is rare.

With the basic analysis clear—or as clear as it can be made in a short time—I now want to extend it to two further points that we must consider before I bring this lecture to its conclusion.

The first point has to do with the good of others, and with our moral obligations toward them. The primary moral obligation of each man is to make a really good life for himself. Unless we understand and discharge this obligation, we are only sentimentalists or thoughtless do-gooders when we concern ourselves with the good of others.

The basic proposition here is that what is really good for me is right for everyone else. Unless I know what is really good for me, I cannot know what is really good for any other man, and unless I know this, I cannot know that he has the same *natural right* that I have to the things that are really good for a human being, each of whom is under the same moral obligation to make a really good life for himself.

The natural rights of other men, based on the things that they need to make good lives for themselves, impose a moral obligation on me, *so far as it is possible, but only so far as it is possible*, not to injure them. I injure them when what I seek for myself deprives them of what they need. *Under ideal conditions*, this can happen only when I seek either what I do not really need at all (such as power or domination over other men) or what I really need, but not to so great an extent (such as superfluous wealth).

Under ideal conditions, the pursuit of happiness is cooperative, not competitive: one man's good life or happiness need not be achieved at the expense of the misery of others, or the ruin of their lives. If this were not so, the pursuit of happiness could not be the basic natural right that a just government ought to facilitate for every human being.

I have reiterated "under ideal conditions." Ideal conditions have never existed on earth, not now, nor ever in the past. In the state of technology in Plato's and Aristotle's day, it may not have been possible for some few men to make good lives for themselves except by the use of slaves—and the misery of many. What is true of ancient Greece, is true of all historic civilizations from the very beginning down to the present day, *in varying degrees*. I shall come back to this point in a moment.

One more question here: the natural rights of other men impose moral obligations on me, *but why should I discharge them?* Since my primary moral obligation is to make a really good life for myself, why should I be just to others, even if I can be? (No one has a moral obligation to do that which, under the circumstances of a particular time, it is impossible to do at that time.)

Put another way: What's in it for me? How does my being just to others (not injuring them) become part of my moral obligation to make a good life for myself? It is easy to see how it contributes to the good life of others; but how does it contribute to my own good life? This is one of the most difficult of all moral questions to answer. I can do no more than indicate the outlines of an answer, as it is developed by Plato and Aristotle.

Justice is the bond of men in states. It is pre-requisite to our living together peacefully, without civil disturbance or violence. Without justice for the most part—if most men were criminals—the state would disintegrate. But each of us needs the state as a means to make a good life for ourselves. Hence in the long run the man who is unjust injures himself. It is only in the short run that injustice to others can ever appear to be expedient. In the long run, the just is always the expedient—not only right, but useful.

Justice to others has its root in the virtues of temperance and courage, concerned with making the right moral choices for the sake of one's own good life. Justice is nothing but these same virtues, socially directed. Hence if a man is habitually unjust to others, he cannot be a man who is habitually temperate and courageous. In short, the man whose virtues dispose him to make his private choices always with an eye on what is really good for himself and on his life as a whole is one in whom the virtues will dispose him to make public choices that do not injure others. If he makes the wrong choices with respect to the good of others, he will also make the wrong choices with respect to his own good.

The second point has to do with the evaluation of societies or cultures. *Are they all equally good? Are some better than others? Or is it impossible,* as the relativists and anthropologists tell us, *to judge societies or cultures without falling into the ethnocentric predicament?*

The ethnocentric predicament? We would be in it if there were no way of judging a culture or society *except* in terms of the value-system that actually prevails in our own society or culture, and may not prevail in any other. If this true, if we are always in an ethnocentric predicament, then we cannot even judge our own society and culture, for when we do so, we beg the question. Yet, paradoxically, the same professors in our colleges who appeal to the ethnocentric predicament, seldom hesitate to pass harsh moral judgments on our own society and culture. Their intellectual schizophrenia allows them to think one way as scientists and as amateur philosophers, and quite another way as dissident or disaffected liberals.

Of course, there is no way out of the ethnocentric predicament unless there are real goods that correspond to natural needs, things that are good for every human being because he is human, without regard to the social or cultural circumstances under which he lives. Only then is there an absolute or transcendant value-system, by which all the relative value-systems—the value-systems that prevail in various societies and cultures—can be judged. And this is precisely what we have in our solution of the basic moral problem, which tells us what any and every man must do in order to make a really good life for himself—the same in its general outlines for all men because each is specifically the same as a man.

Let us now apply this non-relative standard—non-relative because it is relative only to our common human nature, and not to individual differences or to the quite various social and cultural circumstances under which men live. One society or culture is better than another in proportion as its technological conditions, its political and economic institutions, and its actual value-system promote or facilitate a really good life for a *larger* proportion of its human beings. One society or culture is worse than another in proportion as its various components, just mentioned, work in the opposite way—to deprive a greater proportion of its members of the external conditions they need to make good lives for themselves, or to impede or interfere with or even discourage their efforts in this direction.

The ideal, of course, is a society which both provides all its members with the external conditions that they need, and at the same time encourages them in their pursuit of the good life. Under such ideal conditions, it would be completely possible for each individual to make a good life for himself without doing so at the expense of failure or frustration on the part of others.

The point I have been trying to make should be immediately clear with reference to the technological, economic, and political conditions that individuals need for the sake of making a good life—such conditions as health; a maximum amount of free time from subsistence-work; a decent supply of the means of subsistence, certainly above the bare subsistence level; good educational facilities and equal educational opportunities; adequate recreational facilities; freedom from coercion and political liberty; access to enjoyment of the arts; personal and economic security; domestic tranquility and external peace (the absence of internal violence and external war); and so on. But it may not be so clear on the side of cultural conditions: the value-system that obtains in a society may discourage or interfere with an individual's making a good life for himself.

Plato said: "What is honored in a society is cultivated there." Few individuals can be expected to have the heroic virtue needed to be such complete non-conformists that they will seek what they ought to seek in their own lives, against the over-bearing pressure of social disapproval. It is extremely difficult for the individual to seek for himself the things that are not honored or valued in society, or completely to turn his back on the things that are honored there, but wrongly so.

Let me now turn to two concluding questions: Is this a

good time to be alive, and is ours a good society to be alive in? I will deal, first, with our century in relation to all earlier periods of human life on earth; second, with our type of society—the kind that we have in the United States, but which is to be found in many other nations as well; third, with the United States in relation to other societies of the same type; fourth and finally, a few closing comments on those, both at home and abroad, who in various ways and varying degrees express their dissatisfaction with our time and our country.

Is this, our century, a good time to be alive? The answer is unqualifiedly yes. It is better than any earlier period of human life—better in that it provides the external conditions of a good human life to a greater extent and for more human beings than ever before on earth. For the first million to two million years of human life on earth, members of the hominid family led bestial, not characteristically human, lives—that is, they lived mainly, if not exclusively, on the bare subsistence level: two-part lives of sleep and toil. Beginning 35,000 years ago, technological progress began to be made which brought man to the verge of civilization: the domestication of animals, the transition from stone to iron implements, the establishment of permanent settlements, etc.

But not until 6,000 years ago, with the emergence of civilized societies, with superior agricultural technology, with political or quasi-political institutions, with an increased division of labor, and almost always with human slave labor, not until then were the external conditions of a good human life provided for a fortunate and privileged few.

In short, from the beginning to 6,000 years ago, the external conditions for leading a good human life were available *to no one*. Beginning 6,000 years ago, with the rise of cities and civilized societies (which is the same thing), and from then until now—or rather until the end of the 19th century—we have had all over the world what I am going to call parochial civilizations of privilege, based on an inequality of conditions for their human members.

In all these historic, parochial civilizations of privilege, the external conditions of a good human life were provided only for the few, at the expense of misery for all the rest. It seems fair to say that, under the circumstances of the time, especially the poor technology of the time, these inequalities of condition could not have been rectified—except, perhaps, by going backward to a state of affairs in which no one could lead a good human life.

The second great revolution in human affairs began yesterday—with the dawn of this century. The 20th century revolution, which began first in the United States and Western Europe, is now sweeping the world. Please note that I said "began"; for the 20th century revolution has only just stared even in the countries where it first began. It may take anywhere from 100 to 500 years, maybe even 1,000 years, before this revolution yields its full results on a world-wide basis, with the emergence, for the first time, of a world civilization that is based on universal conditions of equality for every human being on earth—*all* men with *no* exceptions.

What is this 20th century revolution? It involves, first of all, extraordinary advances in science and technology, resulting in vastly increased power to produce wealth, in the elimination of inhuman forms of subsistence-work at the level of sheer drudgery, the reduction in the amount of time that must be spent in producing wealth, etc. All these changes indicate that it may at last be possible to eliminate slavery, poverty, unequal educational opportunities, unequal conditions of health, etc.

Second, it involves dedication, in varying degrees, to the democratic principle that all men, being by nature equal, are entitled to an equality of social, economic, and political conditions. It calls for the elimination of all class-divisions, especially the division between the economic haves and have-nots. It calls for political equality—the equality of citizenship, with political rights, liberties, and privileges for all. It is not only democratic but socialistic in that it accepts the principle of the welfare state: that the state should make every effort to promote the general economic welfare, in which all citizens shall participate up to at least the minimum level of a decent and secure standard of living.

This 20th century revolution was first foreshadowed in that single great second paragraph of the Declaration of Independence, which starts with the proposition that all men are born equal, and then conceives the just society as one that will secure to every man his natural rights, among which the primary one is his right to the pursuit of happiness, from which all his other rights flow. But these truths, however self-evident, could not have been realized under the technological conditions of the 18th century. Hence Lincoln's remark about the Declaration, that it was a pledge to the future; and Tocqueville's vision of that future as one in which the revolution that began in America would, under God's providence, ultimately sweep the world.

One need only compare the best country in the world in the middle of the 19th century—whichever one you wish to choose—with a dozen or more states today, in which the 20th century revolution has begun and taken hold, to see that in the latter the external conditions of a good human life are provided for more human beings than ever before on earth.

Let us now briefly consider the states or countries in which the 20th century revolution has begun and taken hold. What characterizes all these states are the following things in varying degrees: political democracy, economic welfare programs, the broadening of public education, public health programs, reduction in the hours of human labor, improvement in the types and conditions of subsistence-work, increase in recreational facilities and participation in the enjoyment of the arts, etc. Let me designate this type of state as the technologically advanced, democratic, welfare state, moving toward, approximating but not get fully achieving, the ideal of the classless society, with a universal equality of conditions and with ample free time for all.

In the world as it is today, we find this type of state realized, again in varying degrees and ways, by: the U.S.A., the states of the British Commonwealth, most of the states of Western Europe (Spain?); and in the Far East, Japan, U.S.S.R. and some of its satellites, especially Czechoslovakia, Yugoslavia, and perhaps Poland; some few states, though to a much less degree, in Central and South America; but not yet to any appreciable degree, in Africa, north or south of the Sahara, in the Middle East, China, India, or Southeast Asia.

All of the states in which the 20th century revolution is now underway and moving forward are vastly superior to any societies that ever existed on earth before—vastly superior to the best of ancient societies, to the Athens of Plato, the Rome of Cicero, or the China of Confucius, in which the conditions of a good life were accessible only to the *very few*.

Now let us consider the United States in comparison with other leading states of the same type—states that are technologically advanced and that have begun to approximate an equality of conditions, politically, economically, and socially. The comparison is difficult to make because it is multi-dimensional. Thus, for example, the United States is much less class-structured than England, has a higher median income than Sweden, has achieved a greater equality of educational opportunity than most European countries, though not more than Australia or Canada, and so on. It also has more political equality and liberty than the U.S.S.R. and its satellites.

On the other hand, economic equality may be more fully achieved in Sweden and in New Zealand; public health may be better cared for in any number of European countries; political democracy may work more responsibly in England; and so on.

With all such considerations in mind, I still think it is fair to say that, from the point of view of providing the external conditions of a good human life for a larger proportion of its citizens, the United States is, *on balance,* as good as, if no better than, any other country in the world today, and vastly better than any state that ever existed in the past.

This brings me, finally, to the adverse criticism of the United States—the complaints and dissatisfactions that are so widely and emotionally voiced on all sides, at home and abroad, by the dissident young and by their disaffected professors, and by the New Left in all its varieties.

In the first place, let me point out that I have said that the 20th century revolution has just begun, even in the United States, and that it has a long way to go before it reaches its full fruitions—the full realization of all the sound principles to which it is dedicated. Hence when I say that the United States is as good as or better than any other country in the world today, I am not saying that it is perfect. *Far from it.*

The war on poverty has just begun; so has the struggle against racism in all its forms. These efforts must be carried forward, and it may take some years to see them through to complete success.

No country is free from the evils of war or the chicanery of foreign policy, and none can be, as long as the jungle or anarchy of sovereign states exist. Foreign affairs is the domain of power politics, and will always remain so until we have advanced to world peace secured in the only way it can be secured—*by world government.*

That, by the way, is the next revolution that lies ahead— the step forward from our parochial societies, always in a state of war with one another, and with an irremediable inequality of conditions as between the have and the have-not nations—forward to a world society, under world government, with an equality of conditions for all men everywhere.

But until that happens, all sovereign states, vis-a-vis one another, are about equally bad; and the United States is no worse than the rest.

The second point I would like to make is that with all its present and past imperfections, the United States has shown itself more susceptible to social change than any other country, has accomplished important social improvements with less violence than other countries, and holds out a greater promise for further positive developments than most other countries.

Hence to call the United States a "sick society" as it is now so fashionable to do, is preposterous if one means by that a society that is mortally or incurably ill. Yet that is precisely what seems to be meant by those whose only aim is the destructive one of tearing down the so-called Establishment, *but without any positive program in hand*.

There is an obvious middle ground between the perfection of blooming health and mortal or incurable disease. And that is where we are—a relatively healthy society with some curable defects or deficiencies. This is the middle ground between the *chauvinism* of saying: my country is right in every way; and the *normanmailerism* of saying: my country is wrong in every way.

The importance of recognizing the soundness of the middle ground in criticizing the United States can be illustrated by the two attitudes one can take toward a house that one is thinking of buying because one wants to live on the site where it exists. Is it so bad a house that the only thing to do with it is to tear it down or gut it, and start from the ground up? Or with all its defects, is it nevertheless good enough to remodel, improve, and redecorate? I say that the United States, with all its defects, is good enough to deserve the second choice—

the choice of trying to improve it by carrying forward the peaceful revolution, reform by due process of law, that has been the course—more than that, the genius—of its development from the beginning.

Let me make just two concluding comments. First, does the prevalent value-system that obtains in the United States encourage or discourage those whom it provides with the external conditions of a good human life to make good use of these favorable circumstances? I am sorry to say that it does not. We place too high a value on the production of commodities, many of which are superfluous for a good life; we place too high a value on having a good time—on sensual indulgences, play, fun, and frolic of all sorts.

This criticism, the kind that Herbert Marcuse, the Pied Piper of the younger generation, has levelled against the technologically advanced society, applies not only to the United States, but to all other states of the same type as well. The complaint in essence is that technology, which should have freed human time for engagement in meaningful human pursuits—pursuits that result in the genuine improvement of human being, not the multiplication of goods and services—seems to have done just the opposite. If Marcuse means, as in part he does, that there is not enough time devoted to play or sensual indulgences of all sorts, he is wrong both in principle and as a matter of fact. But if he means what Lewis Mumford meant years before him, that the increase in labor saving devices has resulted in more human time being devoted to producing and consuming superfluous commodities instead of being devoted to genuine leisure-work, then he is quite right. And all such criticism, on his part or on the part of Kenneth Galbraith who also voices it, has real validity only if it is based on moral principles that would lead them to criticize other aspects of contemporary society as well.

That, however, is not the case. Liberals like Galbraith and revolutionaries like Marcuse sometimes have their hearts in the right place but unfortunately they are unable to put their minds where their hearts are.

The main point I would like to make here is that a moral revolution, not an economic, political, or social revolution, is needed to reform the new industrial state and to turn technological advances into advantages rather than disadvantages. A moral revolution—a fundamental change in our scale of values—is needed to correct the errors of an ever expanding economy.

Some years ago in Aspen, Clarence Randall, then President of Inland Steel, proclaimed that productivity is *the* end of life. The next day, Jacques Barzun and I taught Mr. Randall that productivity is not the end of life, but only one of its means. He may have learned that lesson, but most Americans have not learned it yet. I just said "most Americans," but the point is true of most Englishmen today, most Swedes, most Germans, most Frenchmen, most Russians, and so on. The perverse and corrupt scale of values that is the cultural obstacle to leading a good life in the United States today dominates every other country of the same general type—neither more nor less. Europe is as materialistic as the United States, if not more so.

On the other hand, the cult of sensuality, the addiction to a life of play and frivolity, the existentialist cop-out which consists in living from day to day, with no accounts carried forward—these things are flourishing everywhere, not just in the United States, and it is to these things that the young turn as the only real values when they are disaffected with the materialism and hypocrisy of their elders, not only in the United States but in Europe as well.

What all this calls for is a moral revolution, but a moral

revolution that can begin only after the moral problem is itself understood and the solution of that problem is seen in all its details.

My last point is that many of the criticisms that are now levelled against America and Americans apply to all societies and to the human race generally. All human institutions can be improved, said William Graham Summer; we can remove all human poverty and misery, *were it not for folly and vice.* Folly and vice are human defects, not American defects. Twentieth century America has no monopoly on folly and vice. Nor do those who complain about folly and vice in America have a monopoly on moral conscience.

Plato charged the Athenians who condemned Socrates with folly and vice. The dialogues of Plato are a more penetrating critique of the false values of Athens than anything now being said about America, because Plato, and after him Aristotle, had a true scale of values on which to base criticisms. This is not the case with the present-day critics of the United States, least of all with the most vocal and vociferous young.

The one and only great satire on the human race that has ever been written—*Gulliver's Travels* by Jonathan Swift—would be egregiously misread if it were interpreted as being an attack on 18th century England and Englishmen. It is the great diatribe against mankind that it is because the follies and vices that it satirizes are all human—to be found in every country and at all times because they are populated by men, not by angels or by Swift's gentle rational horses, the Houyhnhnms.

When you listen to the attacks on America and Americans —from our college students and from their professors, or from anybody else—ask yourself whether or not the object of the attack is simply human folly and vice. That is one thing that will put them into perspective. A second thing to consider, to put the attacks or criticisms into perspective, are the kind of facts that I laid out for you a moment ago, in terms of which the 20th century must be compared with all earlier centuries, and the United States with all other countries in the world today. We have not yet achieved perfection, in this century or this country, but we are further along in the march toward it than any earlier century and than most other countries in the world today. This is indisputable. Only ignorance of the facts can lead to the opposite conclusion.

And, finally ask yourselves whether those who criticize their country and their fellowmen have the standards—the scale of values—that would enable them to make good lives for themselves. The evidence is ample, the evidence is overwhelming, that they do not. They are as subject to folly and vice as the objects of their criticism. And the only salvation for them and for all the rest of us is the moral wisdom that must be learned to correct the folly, and the moral discipline that must be cultivated to correct the vice.

THE FUTURE OF THE MORAL ORDER

Paul G. Kuntz

I know that to some of you the moral order seems to have no future. There was once a moral order, but in these days of revolt against tradition and authority, there is only disorder and ever-increasing lack of regularity and discipline. In a state of anarchy there are no limits, and ever increasing permissiveness, as in the arts, seems to foreshadow, as the arts sometimes do, a state of chaos in conduct and relations between man and man.[1]

I know also that to some of you the moral order seems to have had no past. There seems to have been only tyranny imposed by force in which the young served the old, the weak the strong, the black the white, the poor the rich. And the semblance of justification in the name of God and the common good was in the interest of those who had power, meant never to lose it and ever to increase it. Therefore a genuinely moral order seems to be possible only after the decay of the establishment or power structure, or even its overthrow.[2]

Some of you, in the common parlance are "conservatives" and others of you are "radicals," and you may be carefully listening to my opening paragraphs to see if I come forth into the field of battle as a knight of the right to battle the radicals or a knight of the left to battle the conservatives. So which banner do I bear into battle? If I say neither, you may think me a nowhere man without a point of view ("Yellow Submarine" satire about a scholar).[3]

Allow me first to press the advantages of listening to all sides in this debate.[4] Among my five predecessors there has been a subtle dialectic. Two of the papers are descriptive: Mortimer Adler on the present U.S. moral situation and Richard De George on the moralities in the Communist world, particularly the U.S.S.R.[5] It is of the first importance to see that a common principle prevails in these two contrasted systems. Each system claims to work for the benefit of all. Adler says that the American sense of justice is to create the conditions of equality, in the sense that advantages of education are to be made available without discrimination (such as race though he avoids this problem). That is an aspect of our moral revolution. And the principle of the communist system is "from each according to his abilities, to each according to his need." There are deep quarrels about the means adopted in the U.S. and the U.S.S.R. There is rather sharp disagreement about the way to achieve, on one hand, democracy, and, on the other hand, socialism. And each system at the present time is accused of deep hypocrisy. In De George's language, the official moralities do not satisfy the judgment of autonomous morality.[6]

If Adler and De George are appraisers of the social situation of two great world powers, Louis Dupré and Gerald Kreyche are spokesmen for the lonely individual, the man of autonomous morality. I agree deeply with Dupré that our situation in a technical economy is very different from the world of our religious heritage. No longer do we believe ourselves in stations to which God has assigned us. Society is a human contrivance, and what of man in nature? By our science and engineering we have set ourselves to "conquer and to dominate rather than to respect." We do not now regard ourselves as discovering the moral order foreordained by God and with principles established in nature, but rather we are creating our systems of values. Won't our purposes be then merely arbitrary and ephemeral? We are searching for something absolute and ultimate in the universe to serve as ground and principle of our lives. Could it be the devotion to justice to which the founders of our republic devoted their lives (*Federalist Paper,* Hamilton, 51)?[7]

Gerald Kreyche also deals with the individual person who by choice creates values. His deepest need is to be "recognized as a person." Certainly we must agree that there is an integrity of the person and that what we were taught to call "body" and "soul" are better conceived as abstracted aspects rather than as independent substances somehow put together at conception or quickening or birth, one principle from earth and the other from heaven. Certainly we must agree that there is a minimal basic structure of a person's relations to other persons—he binds himself to them by promising to do things, and having promised, is then responsible to do, if possible, whatever he has promised. Here is a principle of the moral order, not imposed upon us by tradition or in the name of God (a command went from Mt. Sinai) and we seem not to be cut off in our innermost reflection from some sanction that seems true without limit of time.

But it is not only man choosing to commit himself to performances in conjunction with other persons. It is necessary also for each of us to make rational choices. There is Vernon Bourke's great contribution—when we make a choice, are we not responsible also to one another to say why we have chosen this rather than that? I don't believe for a moment that Dupré for all his love of Kierkegaard and all his radical Protestant individualism and Kreyche for all his stress on Marcel's individual person would capitulate to Bourke's slashing attack on the existentialist as the arbitrary chooser who makes no defense of the choice other than the sheer fact of having chosen this rather than that.

There are opposite sides in the debate: Dupré and Kreyche

represent the present hostility to Greco-Roman rationalism and Christian scholasticism and Bourke and Adler the voices of that rationalism in the present-day situation.[8]

I am deeply sorry that all six of us did not have the privilege of sharing this platform together for the purposes of dialogue. For, I believe, the oppositions here are tremendously creative of a future moral order. A clash of doctrines is not a defeat but an opportunity. In the name of the concrete individual person Dupré and Kreyche could challenge the very search for an abstract scale of values, such as Bourke seeks (and Adler thinks Aristotle presents). Is it always the case that intellectual satisfaction is better than sensory enjoyment, that given a choice, we should choose the intellectual over the sensory or make the intellectual the end and the sensory the means? The two are conjoined in aesthetic delight so intimately that it falsifies the enjoyment of music and painting to impose this scale upon experiences. There are times when the intellectual is the means and the sensory the end, as when a cook plans a meal, or even more when a priest writes a cook book. There are times when it is not wise to shun the sensory, as though the body were of itself sinful, and the intellect of itself in a higher realm. There may be implicit in such a value scale the old dualism of body and soul against which Kreyche is in revolt.

On the other hand when the individual person chooses, the moral situation Kreyche presents, is this only in relation to other individual persons? In the name of concreteness, why not fill in the picture of institutions in which we live? All of us live in families, in businesses, in schools and churches, in professional organizations... We have a number of "societal codes," as Bourke calls them. Do our choices not follow the patterns of the roles we play relative to each other? Some choices do not fit the institution, even disrupt it. Dupré and Kreyche have left institutional morality out of account. This simply won't pass the test of adequacy to the concrete situation. The human individual person is falsified by abstraction from the complex network of relationships in which we live.

Bourke's point could be restated concretely. In a university we have certain priorities. Although a number of things are good, some are better than others. Individual males must achieve a measure of autonomy, of making up their own minds. One step that is necessary is said to be to say 'no' to their fathers, once or occasionally or even rather constantly to defy their fathers. Now in a university the administrative head, the president, is dangerously exposed as the father image against whom these young males, seeking autonomy, may rebel. Must the university tolerate, in their search for freedom, whatever they may choose to do?

In the jargon of today (which I believe seriously fallacious) the administration is power imposed by the trustees for dark conspiratorial designs to secure conformity. My young rebel friends even regard us faculty member as in the plot to gear young careerists into the military-industrial complex. Is it simply arbitrary for power to punish the powerless students by suspension or expulsion, even arrest and trial for misconduct and damages?

Father Hesburgh set this matter straight in his open letter on campus demonstrations, February 17, 1969:

> I believe that I now have a clear mandate from this University community to see that: (1) Our lines of communication between all segments of the community are kept as open as possible, with all legitimate means of communicating dissent assured, expanded, and protected; (2) civility and rationality are maintained as the most reasonable means of dissent within the academic community; and (3) violation of others' rights or obstructions of the life of the Uni-

versity are outlawed as illegitimate means of dissent in this kind of open society. Violence was especially deplored as violation of everything that the University community stands for.

The alternatives to suspension of the violators, and expulsion also, is a state of anarchy. Forces of law may legitimately be used against those who disrupt the university's paper work.

No one wants the forces of law on this or any other campus, but if some necessitate it, as a last and dismal alternative to anarchy and mob tyranny, let them shoulder the blame instead of receiving the sympathy of a community they would hold at bay. The only alternative I can imagine is turning the majority of the community loose on them and then you have two mobs. I know of no one who would opt for this alternative. . . .[9]

Vernon Bourke well describes our moral thought as that of "a disturbed period of query and criticism" (p. 12). This is particularly important because we need consensus about values in society for society to endure and to develop towards certain goals, even apart from the importance of agreement as one of the tests of truth.

Can we get values established by describing social systems, as Adler and De George do? I believe social science can merely tell us what Americans and Russians say and do. Because the Russians justify the invasion of Czechoslovakia by building Socialism does not make it right. Because Americans seek an even greater G. N. P. does not mean that is the ultimate measuring stick of a great society. Adler and De George clearly agree that a description is not normative.

Vernon Bourke shows us that although we may not look to descriptive sciences for the basis of normative ethics, we should take the situation of man and the nature of man and his institutions into account when we seek out the structures of the moral order. What we need, he concludes, is very much more complex than a simple value scale of intellectual values first, sensory enjoyment second, and biological values third. For one thing "sensory" is too crude—I illustrated it earlier in cooking and in music, but these are very different arts.

Let us consider the situation of man facing not an indefinite future, but more precisely that apocalyptic day, the Year 2000 (twice as apocalyptic as the Year 1000, but less than 1984). The Commission on the Year 2000 was called because of specific questioning of the moral order. Lawrence K. Frank wondered whether Americans can retain a "free social order." The society we have continues to develop under the guidance of John Locke's conception of man and government plus Adam Smith's conception of free enterprise plus, according to most critics, a Utilitarian calculation of the greatest good of the greatest number. The most effective force in giving structure to the society we now have is this set of eighteenth century ideas of a moral order: individual men are free and rational, they join with one another in forming societies including political and economic institutions in order most efficiently to produce the results satisfying human needs. There was a set of strongly held ideas, including self-evident truths "that all men are created equal" and a metaphysical basis of natural law in "nature and nature's God." This was a system including both morality and a great urgency to investigate physical nature and to develop technological control over our environment. If this set of ideas guided our ancestors in setting up the American republic and has guided it since, what may we expect in the next third of a century? Because of the weaking of these ideas, proportionately less guidance and therefore confusion. Because we live in a period when ideas of the moral order change along with changes in the technological economy, we ought to revise our conception of values and goals to guide our descendents as our ancestors helped to guide us.[10]

I do not know whether Frank meant that because we have used an ideology that an ideology must now be used again. If so, this is to be doubted. We have had pointed out to us in detail and with great force that ideologies, as sweeping general pictures of the good society, fail to take account of specific problems. Particularly when they are held dogmatically, they lead to denial of these problems. When we proclaim what the U.S.A. or the U.S.S.R. is supposed to be, we ignore or deny the situations that belie that we have already reached the promised land. In our post-ideological age, as characterized by Daniel Bell, surely the Commission on the year 2000 should have asked whether such a kind of thinking as Sir Karl Popper's "piece-meal social engineering" can take the place of decaying ideology.

"Our values change" is the briefest proposition stated by any of 22 essays in *Toward the Year 2000* and it is a proposition uncontested by any other futurist. The conflict lies in whether there still remains in the American people a consensus about certain base values. Daniel Bell says there remains such a consensus about which values ought to guide us, and the "disagreement [is about] which come[s] first and their exact weights." (Ibid., pp. 667-668). Adler tells us that an industrialist puts productivity as his first value, or to rotate the line 90°, his top value. For Adler productivity cannot be first, for the intellectual and the consumer, steel is a means and not an end. And for anyone we might say that steel would have little value unless used to manufacture other things, unless used in building, etc. Few materials have intrinsic value to the senses, and that would be only one kind of value, aesthetic. In this context we should note that Bell is speaking to Adler's and Bourke's search for a scale of values and replies that there are many scales operative in our moral life.

I shall argue against a consensus and try to use Bell's evidence and that of other social scientists to prove that we do not have any longer a single moral order. We have many moral orders and these tendencies towards fragmentation are likely to intensify. After all, the Commission did not accept Frank's challenge to formulate a set of guiding principles for the American moral order.

In the old moral order there was little doubt about the high value of work. This is now very seriously questioned. After all, admits a theologian of Swedish birth, Krister Stendahl of Harvard University, it was most characteristic of Northern European Protestants to stress "the divine sanction supplied to the high evaluation of work as the meaning of life. Leisure becomes a 'problem' since it is experienced as a vacuum." We have long since ceased to be a WASP culture. The Protestant theologian himself reminds us that according to Chapter 3 of Genesis work is a "curse." The Biblical sanction is gone and there is no longer an economy depending upon the sweat of man's brow." . . . Technology has replaced slavery so as to set men free from full-time work." Moreover we have adopted worthy examples of the enjoyment of what the Greeks called "scholé" (leisure), namely Socrates talking with his Athenian friends. (Ibid., pp. 857-858).

There is no longer a consensus, says our sociologist, that work is good and idleness is bad. There is no longer a consensus, as there once was, about what is private and what is public. (Ibid., p. 677, pp. 876-882). Most important for its bearings on the great guiding ideal of justice is the fact that we no longer accept without reservation the axiom "all men are created equal." What is most crucial is that this natural law belonged to a thought system that stressed man's capacity of reason to grasp the divine pattern of a moral order. That is now in question as it was not for those to whom Isaac Newton had revealed the cosmic mechanical order. What is most crucial is that the human implementation of rational distribution of wealth and control was through the balancing of interests in the market-place and the legislature. Let us see what critical thinkers now say about this set of very familiar presuppositions of our American institutions.

I side with those who say that the belief "all men are created equal" is a prescription that each person has a right to justice, to claim impartial treatment under law. But the zoologist Ernst Mayr takes it empirically as a description. This is a ludicrous misreading of the basic texts. One of them makes it plain that "moral and legal equality . . . make up for that natural and physical difference which prevails among individuals, who, although unequal in personal strength and mental abilities, become thus all equal by conventions and right." (Rousseau's *Social Contract*, quoted, Ibid., p. 704).

Mayr's critique of egalitarianism is complex. It operates on the genetic level, but also on the educational and cultural levels.

> . . . the least desirable aim of all would be to make man homogeneous. Nothing leads more rapidly to extinction than genetic uniformity or homogeneity. If we do any human genetic planning, we must at all times arrange it so that the maximum genetic variability is maintained. Equality in education means setting up our school systems in such a way that each person receives the school's optimal for his individual abilities and eventually finds a job in which he can be reasonably happy and make a maximum contribution (Ibid., p. 677).
>
> Nothing is more undemocratic or more apt to destroy equal opportunity than forcing human beings with exceedingly different aptitudes and motivations through identical social institutions. There is only

one way to cope with man's genetic diversity and that is to diversify man's environment. (Ibid., p. 832-3) Civilization is "achieved by less than one percent of the human population, by those in the upper tail of the curve of human variation in inventiveness, imagination, perseverance, and ability to think clearly. (Ibid., p. 836).

About the Newtonian theistic mechanism, so powerful a cosmology in 18th and 19th centuries, the cosmic setting in which our society and state were moulded, we hear nothing but scorn:

> ... We use the eighteenth-century metaphor 'social forces.' This has become completely meaningless today. What do we mean by it? We are not thinking of large-scale forces that act at a distance. A society is made up of individuals who are guided by values, assumptions, aspirations and feelings. These beliefs and expectations, translated into the various economic, political, social, religious and other patterns and uses of social symbols, direct our social life and provide the dynamic operations that are recorded by these symbols. Let us not be misled by outworn figures of speech and similes patterned upon the older celestial mechanics. (Ibid., p. 672).
>
> And what of "rational utilitarian man?"
>
> Both implicitly and explicitly much of our economic and political thought draws upon the peculiarly rationalistic basis of utilitarianism. Rational economic man in the economists' model is someone who knows what he wants, what his choices are, what his resources are. His value system is assumed to be well defined; his cool, consistent mind quickly and cost-

lessly scans the myriads of alternatives facing him. His flawless discernment enables him to spy subtle differences in quality. He even calculates the value differences between the "giant economy size" and the regular pack. Many an economist realizes, however, that this is not so; that gaps in information exist; that *homo economicus* is not always certain of his desires. Yet it has been felt that the utilitarian model of the maximizing man with complete information is a good approximation. How good an approximation and of what are questions that remain to be answered. As technology grows, markets expand, and societies grow in size, the individual's share of the knowable decreases drastically. More and more the question becomes: How much should one pay for information the worth of which cannot be evaluated until it has been obtained?

Given clear preferences and complete knowledge, rational behavior amounts to following a consistent plan of action toward one's goals. The optimal program may be very complex, but it is well defined. Modern decision theory, economics, psychology, and game theory recognize, as a basic case, clearly motivated individual choice under conditions of complete information. It is also recognized that two unfortunate facts of life remove us from the relative simplicity of this basic case. The first concerns man as an information processor and the second the conflict of individual with group preferences.

Man lives in an environment about which his information is highly incomplete. Not only does he not know how to evaluate many of the alternatives facing him, he is not even aware of a considerable percentage of them. His perceptions are relatively limited;

his powers of calculation and accuracy are less than those of a computer in many situations; his searching, data processing, and memory capacities are erratic. As the speed of transmission of stimulus and the volume of new stimulus increase, the limitations of the individual become more marked relative to society as a whole. *Per se* there is no indication that individual genius or perceptions have changed in an important manner for better or worse in the last few centuries, but the numbers of humans, the size of the body of knowledge, and the complexity of society have grown larger by order of magnitude.

Perhaps the eighteenth and nineteenth centuries will go down as the brief interlude in which the growth of communications and knowledge relative to the size of population, speed of social and political change, and size of the total body of knowledge encouraged individualism and independence. By its very success, this brought about the tremendous need for and growth of knowledge reflected in the research monasteries, colleges of specialists, and cloisters of experts of the twentieth century's corporate society.

And what of the mechanisms of individuals in forming institutions? The atomistic model is simply wrong. "Society is not an aggregate of individuals alone." (Ibid., p. 6) The most incisive critique is not of the free market place (so often pilloried) but of the legislature which is generally uncriticized. Zbigniew Brzezinski is struck by the very conservative ideological formulation of our means and ends. It is not only the Soviets who state their goals in terms of "assumptions very much derived from the distant past." One of these assumptions "becoming irrelevant to our age" is that in making laws we are represented by those whom we elected to legislature and to congress. Thus, in theory, we the people make the laws, and we are self-governing. Are we such in fact, or will we become such in the future?

I would like to suggest at least two basic changes that will be of fundamental importance to the American political system. One is the revolution of the concept of representation. This seems to be moving increasingly in the direction of functional representation, the generalized theory of representation based largely on the predominance of lawyers and generalists giving way to technological, functional specialization. This, in turn, will fundamentally alter the pattern of legislation. Legislation will cease to be a canceling out and balancing of interests, and will become something far more abstracted, involving the weighing of interrelationships within the society and within the technology processes.

Such weighing will have to be done by some body other than that which involves functional representation; by some sort of computing and planning agency outside the legislative process. The legislative process will have to adjust to such changes, and this will in turn pose fundamental problems for the maintenance of the kind of Executive to which we have become accustomed. The expansion of the functions of the Presidency, including the expansion of the personal role of the President, may become something far more symbolic. The President will not be able to adjust effectively and interrelate all of the functional specialized interests that will evolve. Such political problems concerned only with the political system. Unlike economists and technologists, political scientists have not produced any meaningful analyses of change, largely because the political system has become over the last two hundred years a highly conservative institution in relation to social change (Ibid., pp. 670-671).

I am not concluding that the day of rational man is over. Far from it, for the professions and business and government are now dominated by hard working technical intellectuals who master their fields and gain control. The evidence points to continuity of Robert McNamara, McGeorge Bundy, probably the Richard Nixon and Henry Kissenger types, with the American intellectual past that stressed work, reason, and power. But these are no longer spokesmen for the whole people as, for example, Benjamin Franklin once was.

I shall call the morality of the meritocracy "P morality," P for the professions and organizations of professionals who are increasingly powerful, and who, according to some predictions, are bound to dominate and control society. I shall contrast P morality to non-P morality. Sociologically non-P morality is that of non-experts, poets, politicians, humanists, many women, the poor and uneducated. (I am not sure that we will finally be happy with these as a class—but it is only a negative class, in logical opposition to professionals).

This emergence of two moralities is supported by a surprising array of social scientists. Daniel Bell, who has done important work on ideology and education, Erik Erikson, who has done most significant psychiatric studies of human development, Herman Kahn, whose work through the Rand Corporation and Hudson Institute has made him a leading authority on thermonuclear war, and David Riesman, whose *Lonely Crowd* made him the authority on the shift from inner-directed and tradition-directed to other-directed personality in American culture.

The social structure, according to Bell, is going in a direction opposite to that of the culture. The social structure is technocratic, "geared to knowledge and the mastery of complex bodies of learning," in a word, computerized. But "the culture becomes more hedonistic, permissive, expressive, distrustful of authority and of the purposive, delayed-gratification of a bourgeois, achievement-oriented technological world."

Erik Erikson argues a polarization of American youth. There is the humanist pattern, well represented in the existentialist insistence on the individual person. Most of the humanist youth say "that every man is an island unto himself"; nevertheless they stress universal human values. The other pattern, of technology-oriented youth, is so different that they "seem almost to belong to different species." (Ibid., p. 866)

The technologists have little difficulty with the Vietnam War. Like the "hawks" they expect.

> the dominant forces in foreign as well as in domestic matters to work themselves out into some new form of balance of power ... ['Technological' youth] is willing, for the sake of such an expectation, to do a reasonable amount of killing—and of dying. 'Humanist' youth, on the other hand (are like the doves) not only oppos[ing] unlimited mechanization and regimentation, but also cultivat[ing] a sensitive awareness of the humanness of any individual in gunsight range. The two orientations must obviously oppose and repel each other totally; the acceptance of even a part of one could cause an ideological slide in the whole configuration of images and, it follows, in the kind of courage to be—and to die. The two views, therefore, face each other as if the other were *the* enemy, although he may be brother or friend—and, indeed, oneself at a different stage of one's own

life, or even in a different mood of the same stage. (Ibid., pp. 866-867)

Erik Erikson is surely right that coming-of-age in America now is to identify oneself not only positively, but negatively as a beatnik or hippie who is *not* square or as a "neatnik" who washes and is *not* dirty, is well-groomed and *not* long-haired, is well-dressed and *not* sloppy. What will happen to the universalist youth, who in a naïve faith in their moral stance, seem really to believe with Paul Goodman that the problem of the Vietnam War can be solved by putting our troops on planes and boats and bringing them home? Erikson sees a real lack of discipline here that will lead such youth, after failure to move mountains, to retreat into "private worlds" and to form snobbish exclusive cults.

Herman Kahn's analysis links P-morality to Sorokin's "Ideational culture" and non-P morality to Sorokin's "Sensate culture." Kahn agrees with Sorokin that the sensate is winning over the ideational, even though the ideational still dominates government, industry and education. The ideational types are oriented to achievement and these values are mocked by those who see no point in the rat-race of making good which means making money. (Ibid., p. 727)

Kahn is most specific about the fragmentation of the American population into a variety of different moralities. He gives us percentage estimates of each type's importance.

> There is a variation, the scenario of a beatnik United States. Forty-five percent of the population work at their normal thirty-hour work week, nine or ten months a year; 15 per cent work long hours not because they want the money, but because they are compulsive—like the directors of the Hudson Institute, or government people, or intellectuals; 10 per-

cent work short hours because they want to pursue hobbies—painting, skiing, writing poetry, chasing girls, whatever you want; and 10 percent define themselves by rejecting middle-class America—you know, middle-class America is clean, they are dirty; most Americans don't use drugs, they use drugs—the beatnik reaction. I would argue that even though our curves indicate that there will not be very many poor people, America will have a lot of poor people as opposed to Europe. They will be the voluntary poor, the 10 per cent who just accept whatever incomes people have, and then the sociological poor do not get educated, the so-called problem families in what people call the culture of poverty. (Ibid., p. 940)

Whereas Erikson stressed the vulnerability of the non-P morality, its extreme individualism, lack of clear planning, and failure to organize means to achieve definite goals, David Riesman stresses the vulnerability of the P morality. Following the language of Michael Young's celebrated anti-utopia of 1958, *The Rise of the Meritocracy, 1870-2032*, Riesman calls the professional and technological (or ideational) orientation simply "meritocracy." Its danger lies in being too narrow in its search for maximum production and too rational in harnessing all "intelligence in the service of optimal efficiency." The social system is too much under control of the experts who have gained control by merit demonstrated in accomplishment. (Ibid., p. 898)

Riesman's perception of weaknesses in the meritocracy may spell the kind of revolt that Young predicted would bring down the social system.

Meritocracy only appears to have high morale. "It has," says Riesman, no religious base. Is America's romance with practicality and efficiency enough to sustain it? Men serving a system with no goal other than its own further advance have no transcendent aims. They are vulnerable to an inner and outer attack that criticizes them for sustaining a self-perpetuaing structure, rather than helping to cure the meritocratic diseases of society." (Ibid., p. 898)

Meritocracy only appears to be strong in its clear lines of command and its clarity in ranking men on a scale of intelligence from the top of the bottom. Like a salary scale, men are ordered in a single dimension, and of any two different numerical units, either a is higher than b or b is higher than a, and the concept of order is as simple as in Vernon Bourke's value scale: if a is higher than b, and b is higher than c, then a is higher than c. What is the weakness here? Simply that human virtues are multidimensional. When multi-dimensional persons are fitted into a one-dimensional scheme, there is generated a situation against which men must protest in the name of what has been ignored or flattened and straightened out.

There is good reason why Dupré and Kreyche protested in the name of the individual person. Meritocracy is impersonal. The system grades us only according to our efficiency in producing what the system calls for. Your only merit is success in the system's terms, and failure is quickly found out and punished. Most of us are led to protest against the lack of mercy.

In such a system the young who are ambitious, talented, and expert, are quickly forced up the ladder. But in such a system, Riesman points out, they do not develop the character necessary to be leaders. Then too rewards come quickly to the grinds who push away personal and private interests and sacrifice these to the goals of the system pursued with ascetic self-discipline. This produces a protest in the name of charm. (Ibid., pp. 899-901) It has another weakness of the technological intellect: it learns what can be applied immediately or as quickly as possible. It has no interest in knowledge for its own sake, and therefore, has only the narrow practicality that can be outstripped, often in its own game, by broad and speculative learning.

Since the rewards of meritocratic efficiency are external, the motivation to succeed may collapse in disillusion. One recalls the disappointment of the Czarist bureaucrat, Ivan Ilyich, in Tolstoy's great story. The outer world of success is built around an inner void. In the fierce battle for eminent place, the warriors find fewer places that will satisfy them as they rise. In this mad competitive scramble men are easily wounded, and in the end, even a winner feels like a loser. (Ibid., p. 906)

The results of our enquiry into the future of the moral order are far from certain knowledge. But it is a framework in which we can understand the polarization of two moralities. What will happen and when is impossible to predict. But we run the risk of "an ever widening gap between the planners and the people affected by the programs." A psychiatrist asks us to consider the campaign against fluoridation. Is this led by people who are "either unable to understand the information they do get or who are responding irrationally because of the lack of such basic information?" (Ibid., p. 955) The grave danger of polarization is that "a society may become more and more technocratic, more and more rational, and so generate more and more irrationality, since people do not understand the sources of change." (Ibid., p. 955)

The gravest danger that emerges is not only this polarization but the decay of our "public philosophy." This is Walter Lippman's name for the common inherited faith in natural law, individual rights, legal equality, opportunities open to all, public discussion of issues and decision by majority of votes cast. There is so little serious rethinking of our values; men who are supposed to deal with issues tell us about their new gadgets and how bright and shiny they are (John R. Pierce, "Communication," Ibid., pp. 909-921). We cannot look to a commission of experts to replace what has been lost, and perhaps this series of lectures is no more capable of doing what needs doing than was the Commission on the Year 2000.

But I would not wish to leave you with so negative a conclusion: that we face several moralities in the gravest of conflicts. Is it altogether true that each for the other is a devil's morality? In the sense that each says of the other that its maxim is "evil, be thou my good;" this is an exaggeration.

How can two moralities live together? By making themselves intelligible to each other and by developing the kind of dialectical sympathy of a David Riesman who shows that his understanding encompasses both the meritocracy and those who rebel against it. Can we formulate common principles shared by both? If so, we have the basis of consensus that is required.

I do not profess to have the alternative to chaos but I have essayed a sketch of what values bind the professional and the hedonist together.

These four principles cut through the dichotomies that work is either in itself sacred or senseless toil, that equality is either a diseugenic leveling or a claim that each is of equal value in every respect, that one's inner life has no relevance to anyone else or that the common good requires complete control over all parts of society. The four principles I find in both P morality and non-P morality are these:

(1) that it is good to satisfy needs
(2) that life is sacred
(3) that it is right to be honest
(4) that violence should be avoided

I argue these four value principles thus

(1) The professional defers satisfaction, but this is justified only in terms of ultimate satisfaction of need.

Hence the professional does not deny that frustration of need is in itself evil. Would the hedonist, on his part, be willing to concede that his rule of maximizing pleasures must take time into account? Not only must we consider future satisfactions of oneself but also of others and avoid pleasures at the cost of unnecessary pain or frustration of others and pleasures now that have painful consequences.

(2) Is there some common principle of the sacredness of life? Erik Erikson has suggested a desire for "resacralization" and Daniel Bell has suggested, with David Riesman, that some transcendent principle might be implicit in the moralities that will shape life in the future. Perhaps it will not be the divine, as in traditional theology, but the vital, as Albert Schweitzer affirmed in "reverence for life." Perhaps the value of hedonism as a corrective to the morality of meritocracy is that the latter's sacred realm is the rational, that knowledge is better than ignorance, that progressive knowledge is so holy that only sacrifice can be made in its achievement. Bertrand Russell has often suggested that an adequate morality emphasize both love and knowledge, for each alone is partial and inadequate: Love alone is blind and ignorant, knowledge alone ignores interpersonal satisfactions.

(3) Is there any common principle of authenticity? Holden Caulfield in *Catcher in the Rye* rebels against the phoniness all around him at home and at school. When a hedonist discriminates the enjoyable (groovy) from the frustrating (drag) or the indifferent (blah) is he implicitly binding himself to communicate truly with others? In the dealings of professionals with each other and with their clients or patients does the relationship not rest on candor or

honesty or truth-telling? If so, there may be discoverable a common principle of open communication that condemns hypocrisy, deceit, phoniness or inauthenticity that Sartre has condemned as "bad faith."

(4) Does either morality-P or non-P, professional or hedonistic, contain a principle that condemns violence? Does professional morality bind a man to produce a community of understanding based on persuasion rather than on external authority? Does hedonistic morality also, in its social, rather than egotistical form, seek satisfactions that are mutual and shared and thereby condemn violent coercion? If so, we would have a ground for condemning the invasion of privacy. A man's reasoning must be protected, and his development of taste. One morality, because developed in the cognitive realm, focuses on argument, the other morality, because developed in the aesthetic realm, focuses on enjoyment. Either way, one has a principle that protects the member of society from coercive violence and restrains influence within the bounds of persuasion.[11]

I wish in conclusion to leave you with an allegory of finding order in disorder. The human moral scene seems as contradictory as Britain and the United States: in one the driver of a vehicle is told "Bear left!" and in the other the driver is told "Bear right!" And no reason is given other than that tradition and custom so ordain. No axioms to give us a demonstrated theorem and no empirical facts bear on persuading Americans to consider a switch to the left or Britons a switch to the right. We seem equally frozen in our conventionality, British smugness with a tiny minority of countries, American smugness with a vast majority of countries.

Yet recently a nation I visited last summer made the change from driving on the left to driving on the right—Sweden. A commission was set up long prior to September 3, 1967. It found a change was necessary. Sweden was the only continental European country in which British custom prevailed. Swedes driving in Norway and other countries were often involved in accidents, as were Norwegians and other nationals in Sweden. There were difficulties because customs are difficult to change. A third of all Swedes opposed change and some thought of selling their cars. The buses needed right-hand doors and the highway approaches became exits and the exits approaches—not easy to do because cars take more time and distance to slow than to accelerate, so former approaches had to be lengthened. It meant re-educating a whole population, difficult particularly with nomadic Laplanders in their reindeer sleds.

"Driving left" or "driving right" are only low-level values established by custom. These are changeable, relative to time as well as to space. We alter our habits when we drive in Britain, as Britons do in the United States. We have abandoned no good for evil, breached no sacred principle. Quite the contrary: the principle of transportation is to get where you are going and get the stuff there without delay or hazard. So obviously if all vehicles bear either left or right there will be no such likelihood of collision or the anarchy of perfect freedom to go left or go right at whim.

So in our moral order we can recognize a relative aspect like the rules "Bear right!" or "Bear left!" and a not-so relative-aspect, "Get where you are going quickly and safely!" A main task of the future of the moral order is to state where we want to get and how we can get there.

Footnotes

[1] Tom Prideaux, "A Cry from the Past for an Artistic Conscience," in conjunction with "Sex, Shock and Sensuality," *Life*, Vol. 66, No. B, April 4, 1969, pp. 32-34.

[2] Stephen Abbott, "Abbott Raps Bureaucratic Bullshit," *The Emory Wheel*, Vol. 50, No. 18, Feb. 20, 1969, p. 5. I don't so much object to his use of verbal obscenity as the intellectual obscenity of a conspiracy theory because those accused cannot defend themselves by any evidence. Cardinal Newman called this "poisoning the well."

[3] Paul G. Kuntz, "Sir Karl Popper, Man of Ideas," *The Emory Wheel*, Vol. 50, No. 20, March 6, 1969, pp. 3, 8.

[4] Robert C. Doty, "Paul Agonizes Over Dissent Verging on Schism," stresses one of the disadvantages of sharing opposite points of view, *New York Times*, April 6, 1969, Section 4, p. 5E.

[5] On the many social, political and economic systems set up as Marxist, see Milovan Djilas, "There'll be Many Different Communisms in 1984," *The New York Times Magazine*, March 23, 1969, pp. 28-29, 134-137, 140.

[6] Mortimer J. Adler, "The Time of Our Lives," lecture delivered for the Institute on Human Values on March 21, 1969, at Creighton University. (Cf. the fifth essay in this collection. – ed.)

[7] Louis Dupré, "Religion in a Secular World," lecture delivered for the Institute on Human Values on October 24, 1968, at Creighton University. (Cf. the first essay in this collection. – ed.)

[8] Vernon J. Bourke, "Values Scales and Today's Morality," lecture delivered for the Institute on Human Values on November 20, 1968 at Creighton University. (Cf. the second essay in this collection. – ed.)

[9] Theodore M. Hesburgh, C.S.C., "Notre Dame's Tough Policy on Disorder," *The Wall Street Journal*, Feb. 26, 1969, p. 18. Cf. the statement of the American Civil Liberties Union, "A Warning on Student Disorders," *The New York Times*, April 6, 1969, Section 4, p. 6E.

[10] *Toward the Year 2000: Work in Progress, Daedalus*, Vol. 96, No. 3, *Proceedings of the American Academy of Arts and Sciences*, Summer, 1967, p. 664.

[11] A review article "Goals and Values in Transition," based on n. 10, published in the *International Philosophical Quarterly*, IX, 2, June 1969, pp. 278-296. The really hard decisions are when principles lead to conflicting answers. What if some people need violence? What if persuasion does not satisfy them? What if deceit can be used to keep peace?